For Lisbi...
Comrad...
Love,
Jack Hirschman
March 24, 2016

FRONT LINES

SELECTED POEMS

by JACK HIRSCHMAN

POCKET POETS SERIES No. 55

CITY LIGHTS
SAN FRANCISCO

Cover photograph by Edward Brooks
Cover design by Rex Ray
Author portrait by Agneta Falk
Typography by Harvest Graphics

Library of Congress Cataloging-in-Publication Data

Hirschman, Jack, 1933–
    Front lines / by Jack Hirschman.
        p. cm. – (Pocket poets series ; no. 55)
    ISBN 0-87286-400-6
Political poetry, American. I. Title.

    PS3558.I68 F76 2002
    811'.54 — dc21   2002024175

Visit our web site: www.citylights.com

CITY LIGHTS BOOKS are edited by Lawrence Ferlinghetti and
Nancy J. Peters and published at the City Lights Bookstore,
261 Columbus Avenue, San Francisco, CA 94133

ACKNOWLEDGMENTS

"Guerrillas," "Calligraph," "Tornado," "W.C. Fields," "Ikon," "A Correspondence of Americans," and "2 x 4" were published in *A Correspondence of Americans* (Indiana University Press, Bloomington, 1960).

"Three," "Four," "Five," "The Burning of Los Angeles," "Franz Kline," "Jackson Pollock," "Dantesque," "Balaban," "Fugue," "Paris," "El," "Ghetto," "Ray Charles," "The Garden," "Europe," and "London" were published in *Black Alephs* (Trigram Press, London, 1969).

"Hymn" and "Point Lobos" were published in *Cantillations* (Capra Press, Santa Barbara, 1974).

"Let the Railsplitter Awake" was published in *Kashtanya Segodnya* (Beatitude Press, San Francisco, 1975).

"Headlands," "Xleb," "Soul of a Pencil," "Book," "Worker's Poem," and "The Sacrificial Lamb" were published in *Lyripol* (City Lights Books, San Francisco, 1976).

"This Neruda Earth" and "Spirals" were published in *The Necessary Is* (Fishy Afoot Press, San Francisco, 1984).

"NY, NY," "Vladimir Mayakovsky," "One Night," "Mother," "Gardenia," "Haiti," "Ezra Dog" and "Home" were published in *The Bottom Line* (Curbstone Press, Willimantic, CT, 1988) and are reprinted here with their permission.

"October 11, 1990," "Nellie," "Human Interlude," "In Memoriam," "Ray Thompson," "Jesse," "Dancing Dave," "On a Line by Whitman," "When We Tear Tomorrow Open," "Requiem for the War Dead" and "The Night" were published in *Endless Threshold* (Curbstone Press, Willimantic, CT, 1992) and are reprinted here with their permission.

"July 4th Eve 1990," "The International Hotel" and "Wildebeest" were published in *The Back of a Spoon* (manic d press, San Francisco, 1992) and are reprinted here with their permission.

"The Murder of Giordano Bruno" was published bilingually as *L'assassinio de Giordano Bruno* [translated by Antonio Bertoli] (City Lights Italia, Firenze, 2001).

Many of the poems in this book have also appeared in different magazines, journals, newspapers and anthologies through the years: *Alcatraz, Anderson Valley Advertiser, American Poetry Review, Another Chicago Magazine, Ashville Literary Review, Beatitude, Botteghe Oscure, Boumba, Bull Horn, CitiVoice, Compages, First World, Ha Ha Ha!, Gas, Go, Hesperides, Himma, Homeless Writers Forum, Ignite, House Organ, Ikon, Iron, Labor Party Voice, Left Curve, Love Lights, Long Shot, Milk, Moment, New Abolitionist, New Mission News, New Poets of Revolution, Nexus, Northern Contours, Nunzio, One Dog, Onthebus, Open City, People's Tribune, Poetry Now, Poetry Roundup, Power Lines, Promethean, Ragged Lion, Rain City Review, Southwest Review, Split Shift, Streetsheet, Street Spirit, Stump, Temper, Tenant Times, Tenderloin Times, The Bomb, The Café Review, The Hammer, The Haight-Ashbury Literary Journal, The Haitian Information Bureau Newsletter, The Outlaw Bible, and Urban Love.*

To My Gentle Comrades

CONTENTS

FRONT LINES

GUERRILLAS

In the mountain caves they sleep:
The Stubborn Men.
Without the quench of water,
Without the warmth of woman or child.
       Bedpost of bayonet,
       Pillow of steel.

1952

FOR DYLAN THOMAS

That wind, that wind of water vowels
Whirled from the singing bones
Of him who reaped a world of music
In the throat's harp, and sainted heaven
In the grottoes of the ear,
Raptures me yet, fans with bellowing flame
The woebegone blood, and cancels
Elegy in the mourningband night.

That pen, that pen sprung
From the poetry of seas, has scrawled
Bibles of a child on rusted leaves
And made them fly,
Has slashed the curtained anarchy
Of crippled sound and cryptic word,
And swallowed empty scriptures
In the deluge of its breath.

That death, that death, the crumbling
Of a brain, the mouth whose issue
Made the stained glass holy
While cold November rain rapped fate,

I do not lament.
For in the poverty of days, I am swollen
By the fullblown cantos, from the mouth
Of the choir of the bellringing dead.

1953

20

CALLIGRAPH

for Ruth

Her hair hysterical, thrown back at the sight
Of the rose my throbbing boyhood brought,
Incensed, how the man in me leaped from my blush
And struck a trembling smile upon her mouth,

And how, drawing a tattered kimono close,
With fingers soft as pounded paraffin,
She bent and lifted up a thin-necked vase
To put the fiower in.

1956

4

TORNADO

Amid shambles blown, blown pages of a Gideon,
A farmer with a pitchfork stepped
Before the microphone and said it was a huge
Black arm did it, come sweeping across
The tabletop plain, grizzly, on a binge.

His wife, kind of scared and something shy
Of things stuck right before your face
To talk into, was in the distant field
Pecking at the wreckage of a moviehouse
Fallen out of the sky, for pans.

And still agog, the kid in overalls
Was dancing on shingles, leaping
From tree to tree, his blond crop fluttering,
Yelling to all the buried farmboys
About the swindging tail of the dragon that snapped.

1956

W.C. FIELDS

By Jove, my glowworm dove my chickadee Death's
Caught up with me at last with the last billing,
And so many elegant days are still unsipped.
'Tis a fraud, I say, 'tis a fraud; 'tis fraught
With imminent danger, the coming of this fellow
In the bright nightgown.

Drat it, goodbye stuffed fowl of a life foreshortened,
Goodbye rim of the glass of pure water forlorn,
Goodbye blond pulchritude of farflung travels,
Sunflowers I shall not sniff, balls not juggle,
Goodbye. In a moment rather I shall endeavor
To climb the wagon whose steeds will wend
Bumpily along the road's parched tongue
To the provinces.

But, Jehosaphat, my good man, has the chef
By some mischance omitted the paprika?

                                        1956

6

IKON

of Allen Ginsberg

His howl grabbed me by my high intangibles;
His humor, of the ghetto-American, riddled
Me silly as Fosdick of the cops,
My gassy dialectic escaping to be filled
By dancing inbetween despairs, and flops.

A cloud in trousers baggied by the wind
I came down the musical chute to find
In a riff-raff flat, a pock on the cheek
Off the stumblebum-bandaged nose of the Bowery,
A kind of a poet and a humankind of skin:

The frockcoat face with its curling sleeves
Of raskolnikovian-rivington weave,
Then the horned spectacle of his eyes, a cross
Between the visionary and mission bum-boss,
So shoulder-drooped they kissed across his body;

And a kitchen as shambled as the czarina's
My grandmother's slum, whose bulbas
Bloomed in the potted beds, and every bed

Grew a plot of hysterical revolution as
The sons of the gunsel slept.

We sat, we talked over crumbs while a roach
Shuttled like a brown monk to and fro
Across the thread unwinding tongues spelt out,
Tottering this way, with whispers of my host
And, with my host of praises, that:

Shrug which kept our balance and composed
An hour's ease between my eyes and those
Of the invert in the apocalyptic rant
Who swaddled a century burning in his thighs
And tousled the strings of its dying instruments.

From his hands I saw that he
Was in a perpetual state of litany;
Between the thin blue lines of lips
I could almost read with fingertips
The wine-drenched letters of a race
Driven across the tragic page
Incomprehensibly with laughter.

Here was no perfection of tongues
But a babel apprenticing;
Confounded and blasted young, what

If whatever came up spat out of throat?
Dimestore prophetics at best, and yet,
With "the everlasting eyes of Charlot
And, of Gargantua, the laughter,"

I felt our words promising to become
Huddled buddies under the bomb,
Learning like Fields and Marc Chagall,
Yeats and Finnegan and all that fell
From the first into the human tense
To scramble to their feet and dance
Circles round the crater,

Billowing across the dazzled sky
Benignly tender zeppelins of a smile,
Signature of all things yet to come
When the light fades and we lay down
Drumbeat and intellection's scars
And wake to name the things around by heart.

1957

A CORRESPONDENCE OF AMERICANS

I

I miss those free-wheeling interborough rides
Of minds lit up through the tunnels
Where we were palely cast, and the less widest, wide
Spin and descending sift of puns down the funnel

To shuteye purgation: of the Deuce of Heads
Put together and become the one and only King Jam
Boxed in the dark age of a die and rattling ahead
Of our time Jimjack, jimjammed, jammed

In with the comicstripped faces and the frumps
Plush from soft broadways, closing, where Kid
Mulligan just happening by offered his stump
Tapping pennytunes, ponderous upon our lids.

I left it, boy, and you, end I say endlessly riding
The rails riding nowhere, shuttled for a freight
Somewhere, America, bound, with a weddingbond
        guiding.
So cleanly damned, my weeks are like the old iambic feet

Out here, limping toward their sabbatical ends, I say
Endlessly limping. And healthfully, unsicklied unto death,
With a biblebelt to keep my trousers up and lots of space
To hold my follies in, and a twanged American Gothic
        breath

That frequents the local tornado haunts, vainly urging
From darkness a vision of trembling hands emerging.

II

From afar, this day you brandish a bride, Dear Jim,
I gift you a handful of wishes (stop) that godhead,
The unutterable vows we made to die in need of him
Forget: his limbs are broken (steps) quite dead.

(Where you are tomorrow already is, as shadows go
Easy up over the gotham we trod, westwardly ho,
And the sky is cathedraldomed like a stained blue
Eyelid closed upon a benediction of you.

Farrer now, the negroes minstrelling waters behind,
I am dawning too and stretching reflection from toe
Bent as coastlines bend embracing trades and tides,
To the badlands of my face forefathered into stone.

And her galloping, spur-hysterical mane of night
Fallen loosely like blond towns among the grain,
Resolves all differences, and the votiveness of eyes
Uplifted on the bicepped hill), dear Jim, a gain

Of boys it was, no more, a fungo's soft preliminary
To play. (Steeped) now, no less than ever I be for her
Sugar in hand, rod, snake underhoof, dad, coming to her
As the lore of the land, widespread as sodomy.

III

Level, yet, your sculptural profile was with mine
Mounted high across the rivers of coffee spilt:
What volume we raised, divinity, was our divide,
Though close as one can come, we came, to guilt.

Like the flies that ate philosophies off our lips
Cactuses on the moonsplayed desert fret the mind,
And the rhythms of the streets we knew outside
Were splintered, tropical pick-up sticks,

And the nights, above all, the spaces complementary
In our eyes. Now nothing is before me, and behind,
The tense of fossilized hoofprints and the weary
Pilgrims' stop, as if they had been beaten into wind,

And I move as the metric in a poem whose theme is ruin,
But more than theme or metric the poem is a ruin,
Fractured by handling cracked by time and weather,
Whose darkness is doomed henceforth to the scholar

Who'll appear with incisions of pen where, knelt,
At the edge of new waters, giantstep-trodden, I,
And peck at and pick out the message that spelt
The invisible twin opposite these arms would edify.

IV

At the extreme end something beginning is sown,
The last cablecar not chattering to its stop
But stopping to start up and clattering down
Hills like an old tune become apocalyptically bop.

So it was, the moment after the sudden earthquake
Astonished their downfalls into shatterglass toasts:
Hands fumbling into pockets fumbling with the shakes
For butt-ends to rebuild the Barbary Coast.

It all reminds me of. The same face, Love, ever
Changing and anew. The man who planted bombs
Last Christmas in your eyes, I've seen the blossoms
Up through schisms breaking; and I know howsoever

The whirr of planes approaches me, dearer by far
They are actually approaching you. Overshadowing
Unto. Like a lip I'd lay upon yours, silencing,
While wide baywaters lap trinities, heart to heart.

But I am: Fog horn, calls from low dives. Gulls cry
Above my cry. Overshadowing you too. Fag on fag
Lit up at the extreme end of. Something, a cry
I am, beginning to be fogged. Far gone and gone on jag.

V

Our images, Jim, have come to the ice
Left in once drunkenly lifted cups.
In the slow dissolutions, crystal clear,
Faces are staring, of infinite failure, up.

You at the other end of the inevitable bar
Extending crosscountry, the picketed harbor
Of your eyes; and, picketed, I at the other,
And inbetween all our mad specters:

The tenors intertwined, the widening forever
Frontier song like the future tense of dreams
Unlimited. O it's dissonance now, but listen,
I'll stand you one and then you'll one for me

And one by one well topple down the ghosts
To the gay center, where I'll say to you:
'Lean against me with your irreligious brogue
And I will lean the shoulder of a Jew,

Sagging as a smile, and stagger with you
Past the stoned fictions of ourselves as gods,
Out of these swinging doors, this omaha nowhere,
Bound, for all space, nowhere, clods.'

1958

toward down

No longer the singular we two wedded in bedrock,
The simple conjugation of our love has given way
Anatomically to forms that have eroticized the shock
That in sharing our decadence decadence decays.

The path we once knew, immediate to our senses
As a rose within a thin-necked vase,
Deviously sinistral we've wandered and demented
In the ultimate light, ultimately base.

by day

The night persists. The fictions held between us
Curl and grow frayed in their neglected bindings
As our fingers play past them on another corpus:
A young American suicide, the intricate windings

Of a derelict through boyflowering Alexandrine
Streets, ryder and nightwood and the ghostly loves
Of a woman not yet risen from her sleep, Justine:
The palpable pithed strings the mind is soundless of.

tonight

I lay beside you and you were whore
To my touch, and boy I craved but never could approach;
In the shadow of your neck I became the pale boy before
Me, and the girl, at your breast, open as a broach;

I lay with another woman and yet
With whom within and against what cheek I cannot say,
I cannot say anything, as we kiss, that's past, except
The thrilled breast at my tongue I will not betray.

and now

In this 2 x 4, tender on down to the soft breathings
And the cigaret passed as a metronome commenting on,
Should you turn to me to touch and find that something's
Come between us; should your fingers tick with agitation,

Tense, and cross with mine your wrist, and where
The furious strum is, I will, even as my lips erode,
Lobe with a kiss more global than the world your ear,
And whisper, when you whisper, what we're coming to,
        God!

1959

17

THREE

The tree outside the window,
when I look again it's spring,
and this room of our in-fighting.

Meli meli's greek for the honey
your hair, it was
bourbon in winter.

Changes, the laughing, slip-
ping out of things,
and the way we spring in each

other then, lush and green
and later still with
my finger on

the form of which
the seasons are
expressions like:

Are you done?
I'm aching.
Come here.

1960

FOUR

You come into a white room
the way brushstroke
enters my eye,
defines me

'Tall, and of a port in air.'
I take the line of another
written about a jar
and put it to your ear.

The sea, the sea is in it,
and it was empty until
you turned to
drink from the lip of it.

Now it lies still, on its
side your wild strokes,
so many memorables,
drying.

1961
28

FIVE

You move from a repose
I am far behind,
and vain.

The simple way you
take things in
that are, after all,
trembling.

Two years ago I was
a Lublinjuggler,
a Dublinjew last year
was I.

Since you have put
your finger on me
I have no desire,
no more water in

the pail, no more
moon in the water,
only this snow
falling, this

slow filling up of
room.

1961

IN MEMORIAM ERNEST HEMINGWAY

Lightning-runs down the midnight
dakota sky.

We slept in back of the wagon, feet
stuck out of mosquito netting.

It was hot.
Wy-

oming in the morning was indian-
red with ax-nose mountains of

Shoshone, chin-cliffs of sediment
piled high and telling of

                when mountains fought
                each other and
                Big Horn narrowed
                with clay and silt
                to

montana browns and greens. Bucks loping
on hills, wilderness bear,

a great tree growing out of the head
of a moose.

We headed south in Idaho, riding clear
of towns, taking back roads, filling
the back of the wagon with sprigs
and flowers.

Never turned the radio on.
Never read a headline.

We hit California. The newspaper said,
Papa, you were three days dead.
The cities and towns piled up again.
The sun got blinding. She put on dark glasses.

I drove slowly through the streets to the end.

1961

THE BURNING OF LOS ANGELES

Smelled her before the eyes saw her
    going east from the sea on Sunset
got a whiff of her through the smog valved exhausts
    nagging motor grind of the winding road
She was lining them up for miles at the pass
    of the freeway under me

Supple up there licking the tops of the trees
chewing the hair offa them
    A deer came down a canyon with
      a piece of her and done
    A palomino came down his mane was her and died
at the edge of the gutter
      with jacarandas died with cries
of muskrats leaping from trees
thumps of rabbits on stone
                Screeches and whine of
sirens of engines ambulance spotlight
out of the awe of my eye

Broke into a cold run diagonally across my legs
    in front of me up a canyon drive

She smelled deeper the closer I came natural
       red white and black
The higher I ran Man against wall upon roof
       with piddling garden hose
A colt in agony by I never looked back
And she'd bitten the wrists and calves of a poodle
       and three other bitches who ran from the heat
could see her slithering a thigh against a rooftop
More and more trees saw her blowing black
       and blue through morning smoke a hole of sky

They were coming down down away from her nails her
       teeth cadillacs jaguars a chauffeur
         in profile what wildness of laugh-eye
And a moose with the body of a man came running down
And a trophy she kissed one side of the sun gone tar
       black bellies of pillows with goosefeathers
and jewels stuffed Picasso
ran right passed
            Renoir

Crazy it was dada with czars and jews both gritting
       with bitten cigar-ends angry cuts
A couple kids pointing Wow, she's nekked
The cops thick around

                    the spouting engines
clubbing her hard nails banging her ankles cops
with boys at the corner of their mouths wanted her
hip to hip cops with
                           handmedownhose
cops nada cops nuns in pairs gasmasks to keep from smell
her rich armpits the mole in the middle I hide in
dry brush watch them spit
at her bite at her paw

And how she fumes and fangs back booms windily from
        inside a house spits billions of windowglass shells
Rears up like wall water falls upward by the santana whips
            the fuzz on their cheeks with cycloon gives
            them wilderness eye throws back
her hair blasts their faces with blush says
                C'mon you cn do bettern that, says
                Why din't ytell me at the edge, says
        This is no place for kids, bends

And scatters them so many pins with one roll and uproar
        of a fireball and I light I light up
            right then and there
                    we're alone no sound but the sirens
        and spittle high back in her throat

She's smelling me out she's not saying No she's not
      saying Yesbut she's not saying anything but
        lean I can see her
        step out of brush
            window lean up against Wall
      light up the corner of her smile a
        click of sheer mesh of
          stocking of sullen
            backless heels clacking
Time it was
        Time on high street with the great again
grandmother of every whore gig sweet you
And she laughs a whole stable of
flaming bluebloods spill foaming whinneying out
veining down the canyon a carpet of
      meat for my leap
      And I leap

               1962

FRANZ KLINE

Wanted to paint. Come
out of coal country to New
York wanting to paint. Painted
everything he saw: El trains,
pushcarts, the insides of
bars. Paint. Paint. Paint.
Got to know the feel of New York,
the up and down, the somber
up and down, the looming
vertical of steel and face
and bone. Sometimes he'd throw in the
light more than bleak, the gold almost
white. Mostly it was browns and mauves,
huddled old worsted saloons, the
lower east side fog.

Then one morning his heart stopped
thinking about painting, painting
about feeling. Without his knowing
it had stopped, it stopped thinking
about painting feeling. Stopped.

He was hungover. He went to the sink
and washed and found himself clean.
He sat on the bowl and felt himself
emptying coal bones faces buildings
ramps cries laughs loves everything.

It was then he began, for a very brief
time given him, *not* to paint these
absolutely simple
accidentally mastered
blacks and whites
looking at you as no man might
taking off his clothes,
as no window is facing yours
200 stories up,
as no tree in a countryside
is smiling at the passing comments

1962

JACKSON POLLOCK

1.

He met it straight
met it empty,
the white of its eye
the space that was longing,

made it wait, sized it
up to the height of
his head, to the breadth
of the only thing certain,

his body, the depth of
his senses mixing,
stirring, peered over
the rim of, down the long iris of

It, leered down and roared
at himself looking up and
ho danced Him streaking
whatever came to brush,

riptooth bits of glass slurs
of this moment only
in this color clumsy big
oafed or obedient thin

as the wrist singing This
is the making of It—
and signed with the flair of a
boy his name

to this ideogram meeting
me head on
at the speed of his own
cut tendons.

2.

It is a continent of sky and sea perdita,
star-inscape upon fishglint superimposed,
the first house of a zodiac he has made
of the cool moon on your body, Roshima
        I asked the ten shadows
        on Yorozuyo-bashi Bridge.
        They said it was so.

Moreover there are women who cannot have
her child anymore. We may not say of
future ones like as influence to embryos.
When everything ceased to exist at once,
  they said, they remember
  him feeling for skin
  as a blind man
  sorrows.

I am moved by rhythms I no longer understand
nor want to want to,
home as I am here in what is yours, what you've
given mankind the constant praising passing through.

3.

The moment it met him head on
he knew death was a hand
he must shake,
and it slapped him down

in the sentimental bounty
of the roadster, stretched
him on the screaming
brake white as canvas,

made him see the last
ritual of himself in
poles slashing by in
the moonlight, clotted
the sky of his mind with
golden egg bursting
his bicep the mountainous
lavish and roll of

a map of, of a land with
arteries lashed and
unleashing
the flush kept back,

the strain of the whole
engine riveted on
becoming
easy again

as a line is, rounding
the wheel, its eye
dead white in the center
he spatters against.

1962

DANTESQUE

for Rico Lebrun

A man ran up to me and cried, Dante
is dead. I said,
of course.
He said the hearse was

coming down the road, get
up. I said no,
of course, and made
the sign of the cross

as he begged. When his body came over
me I reached up
hugged it
was dragged

how many years you can guess
to a pit at the edge
of town. I had grown
older, my sex

changed in the embrace. I
felt like Lucia

33

bearing him
up to Beatrice.

Of course you know the rest.
The pit was full of Jews.
The hearse backed up, they separated us.
And away we flew

1963

THE MURDER OF GIORDANO BRUNO

(February 19, 1600)

Prologue

He began to heaven
happy there was nothing now to do but die
simply
      open eyes as the bars clanged
      behind him
              Seven years behind him
              All his
                  life's stars' wandering over
      Europe, come into this
      Campo di Fiori
          He is naked
san benito
painted with flames and devils

            The hag cries, market gabble
still within earshot
            of the Ave Caesars

dying with the dying
gladiators,
                    of Caesar
himself dying with his
'Et tu,   Brute?'

    He is bound.
    He is asked
                    once more to kiss
                    the (redhot)
                    cross
Who will not recant, who may not recant,
who has nothing to recant, nor
reason to recant, nor
knows what to
                Recant
                    turning his lips
                    away, closing
                    his eyes there, now,
                    the better to see

            •   •   •

The flame kissed his feet
the kingdoms

walked over, the chestnut
hair but a shrub on
his chin pointing
                west out of

(dear little) Nola now in mind
       The first
       space of meadow and river

       where he saw
                   How many, how much
      she had given

The moon in the water by night
The moon at his window
The moon like a coin
on the shoulder
         of Vesuvio.
         Different.
         The same.
                Younger as older

           •   •   •

The flame kissed his crotch
as the flame

when he fled cloister
and the capes etched
along the coast
knew him
                    The sweet prison then
between mountain chains
where he'd sit, overlook,
  remember
                    kidney mountains,
                    great lakes of liver,
                    the tigres-euphrates
                    network of heart,
                    brain and seed a
                    strange cotyledon,
                    flowers and grass sweet
                    fingers
Each
    its own center, each
    interpenetrating
                    infinite atomies,
                    and the heart
                    of the sun
                    he looked in
                    the eye, was it
                    any more center

                    than the heart of
           the ant crawling over the
           empty white leaf
                         words would be
                    written on

                    •   •   •

The flame kissed his left thigh
The firmness
                    with which it went, lamenting
                    through intestine-torn
                    France, the Seine
                              one bleeding gore of wound
      His tonsure,
      his manuscripts
                    undercover of
                    secular cloak
                              Suspect.
                              Banished
        from the university
        for teaching :
                         Each sperm a potential
              sun.   That sun
                         dark with blood, but

                    the shadow of another

        And no more center
        than the center

                    This child
    screaming down the road through the pestilence for

            "Mother!"

                            is
                            everywhere

                    •   •   •

The flame kissed his right thigh
The splendor
            of its hard stride down
            on English soil

                    The friends there,
                    the haven for
                    his beard full
                    of dried spittle
                            not to be tweeked there

                    40

Among the tall minds, but

        the Sciences galloping
        down the cobbles
        protesting so vehemently
        with bite, strained muscles

O dumb runaways
                with blinders
        not seeing what
            overlooked stones kicked up
                        by hoofs
Sparks
        in the black of the earth
        while they streak
                headlong by
                furlong

                    The carriage torn from,
                    the reins
                            worn
                            thin
                into the animal centuries

            •   •   •

The flame kissed the beauty
of his heart
        The still contemplation
        dangling from
        the cemetery wall
        at Wittenberg
                The last lecture given
   And thought of home, of

        Nola, the closest shadow of

Home
        That student prince
        who asked the question,

        that strange young light
        so much himself, all

        eyes in the lecturehall
        turned when he spoke

                (A shadow
                of home)

:'If the sun breed maggots in a dead dog,
  being a God-kissing carrion . . .'

The beauty of the soft
irony of his voice

Sol et homogenerant hominem

. . .

The flame kissed the power
of his mercy
                    Now traveling faster
                              Prague
                              Helmstedt
                    His body feathering

          O this was
                         It
                              lighter even than his thought of

                         It
                              first come from the prison

. . .

The flame kissed the majesty
of the bulk of

his works

      restated in Frankfort
      with an anxious rush to be

                (Dear

                    little)

      Leaves upon leaves
      so thinly
      veined

         In their most minimum
         Most High

        •   •   •

The flame kissed his right shoulder
      All intelligence buckled
      before/ All his bitterness
      with the years after
      Moncenigo that dog
      and Venice of dog's
      piss, the trials and
      dungeons, the dark
      visitations
         Who now?

Who now?
                    To wring

        Recant
                    O
Christ, the piazza truly flowers

            .   .   .

The flame kissed his left shoulder
                    had eyes, saw
                    wisdom belonging to
            saw
                    CHOKMAH
            had hands as well, touched
            the black letters
                        biled,
            had lips as well, bent, kissed
            the letters had ears, heard
                        himself called:

    Philosopher.   Chokmah.
    Come

            .   .   .

45

The flame kissed his crown
                opened
                his eyes in white fire in black fire

        He is sound
        He is script
        He is number
                        entering soundless
                        thinning imageless
                        zeroing numberless

            Still

                        •   •   •

                                    1963

BALABAN

I ran down the street and into the house smelled
of oregano and shook Mickey Monaco, said
C'mon, Balaban's got a breadloaf
climbing over old Gruber's fence, he thinks
the mad dogs is doves.

But Mickey grew up in the bed till he was too old
and besides Balaban was crazy, he sucked
his tongue and got left back twice.

So I ran to Joey Bellino's house but his mother's
black stocking said Joey was out early shoe
shining. And besides a, that Balaban he's a
crazy a kid, he suck a the tongue and Joey says
he get lefback three times.

So I banged on Bitsy Beller's window yelled he was
near the top, the mad dogs waiting down
below he thinks is doves.

But when Bitsy stood up he turned into a stiff
cue stick. And didn't want nothing to do
with nobody cracked upstairs.

And Dickie Miller became a semipro. And Howie Fish
a doctor. So I ran down the street full of hope

by myself because I was on fire. But I got there
too late for Balaban. Two of them had a stretch
of skin between their teeth fighting over it,

and the foam of their mouths and Balaban's blood
spattered in such a way, the most the greatest
picture looked me straight in the eye, made me
sit in the gutter and cry,

and when I got up vowed to be
Balaban from that day on.

1963

HYMN

I am at home,
you are at home,
inside

the children are
asleep in
their room

inside, I am
working
under

    The Lamp
    of the
    poem

1964

31

FUGUE

To the beloved
                memory of Johann
                                Sebastian Bach
        and in the emptiness
                of form and to no purpose but
        to name a beloved
                        who is dead and living
        music by memorial
                inspiration of
                        Johann upon
                                the organ
in the emptiness
            of the church of
                        St. Sebastian
                at the key
                        board of Being
            empty
                at the full
                        strength of his
                        form to no
                purpose but praising
                I praise

Thee
    Bach bastion
        beloved
even of
        saints.

1964

PARIS

Through the window from inside
the cafe is in the street
the trees are in the cafe
the silver espresso trees
a couple is kissing under
the outside of inside
the soft yellow lights
in the gutter cafe
Ray Charles is singing
Georgia on the jukebox
at the corner of
Rue Delambre
inside the cafe
Wallace Berman comes by
and frames it and calls it
America
and gives it away.

1965

EL

The room was dark but not yet black
I took her there her hair all wild
with bourbon bourbon on the mind
I lay her down her liason dark and
not yet black with distance took her
thighs and spread them wild and wide
she wrapped me as she had and made
her whisper as she had him in
the room was dark but not yet black
riding until she called me stallion
I called her cunt and slut and slide
I broke her into books of dead mishnah
with all the various changes tried
heaping up broken letters and charred
bodies of moans and groans and crying
hatreds grew hills of hair multiplying
and still out of reach the black fire
she was in the room beyond her burning.

1966

GHETTO

Men fight. With their fists in the balls of their mouths
in the silences between they bitch out their boys. At
the shabby corner store they cut each other to ribbons,
stand up skinny pricks against the damp mackinaw wall
of skyblue chalkstick death in Kingsbridge in Fordham
      down
at Hunt's Point in Pelham I pass through three and a half
room hands my profile still set against the black girders
and rattling trains, my dark books still scared of the shiv
and rumble of Jerome and Elder mira mira my face at Bath-
gate Freeman they are dropping sensations out of the
      Daily
News trucks I have attacked an eight-year-old boy in the
ruins of Starlight Park near the bones of the Coliseum
and the cheeseboxes with cut-out eyes open into the anger
of housedresses all inscribed in corduroy terror by a left
back with tongue slobbering somewhere in the upper
      reaches
of his gums on a blacksatin Friday night a cellardoor o-
pening to the sky import strictly from Harlem is muffed
on the cushions by a million pimples. And this my
      chassidic
teacher is where I go back to begin from. Na, share this

dead bowl of kaddish we go downtown:

       black island ghost blocks at dawn drubbed
stumbling hypnotic cold hungover and eerie,
       his pride sticking out of his sock her face
kissing Jerusalem's early suicide on East 33rd on Bleeker,
       my broken bottleneck for kill,
       my paperbag sherry,
       black dada nihilismus wizardry of the kissed
ass,
       tomorrow's loot music,
       all the evil haberdashery of roach fingers
crawling all over the whites of their eyes,
       sewers lined with dynamite,
       vein streets junk bulletholes in the rock island
arm sucking animals at midnight,
       eat the heart of massa and throb Kong,
       beat hisself to death and die alive man the
                       screaming
next door will you shut up for chrissakes,
       Bird is walking on the waters of piss,
       gutter hoarse and fogged with slush affections,
       The Trane is setting,
       she stink the summer armpit the winter burning
cold compassion,
       she tell me to my face gutter you go out and

get a coat,

    she bang on my rib radiator wake up to the
black sun,

     with tired shoes she springs

Who showed you the rot in the ring and smiled fear?
Pointed to jail and bawled at the bars of your freedom?
Put the blear and round of this world in your eyes
so that only the shades and the shadows would do?
Taught you the motherfuck? beat hell
out of night so you finally could get some shuteye?
Bum. Scuffle. Before and behind. While your mother
was having a heartattack and your old man my foot
went shellacking the sidewalk in search of an
eight-ounce mitt he could call the pride of his son?

     Golem
       me make you bitter
     sweet numbers and letters
       dialed to a hundred no's
    from the rotten heart
      beat you ate
    —conceited!—
    out of garbage cans and crumpled
    teachings
    out of the bratty insolences

of the old and young alike
out of hooey and dig the bam the
crack the jerkoff
under the yellow bulb beside
the tarnished mailbox and warped
green paint of the door always
slamming behind the elevators too
cramped or bowls with the retch of
the wretched
                    come
                              to your teeming
shores to raise a John
    who be my just disciple
              Golem
          assassinated Golem of
                    war Golem weary
              Golem pitiful
              Golem juice is all
run dry and goes on speed and goes
in drag
      Daddy Warbucks pileup
          Muscle hanging limp
      at the beginning and the end of all
          Our Brag.

                    1967

RAY CHARLES

Sat down on a bench in Venice late November of the war
with my kid's transistor radio at my ear you sang Yesterday
sweet and withdrawn without teeth through the gums of
      Dak To
old man of the blind dark days old solo singing through
      mob
who shouted Yeah to me in Paris shouted Yeah to me in
      Greece
born loser shouting Yeah in London in New York across
      the board
jesus they come up quick and the wheels spin goddamn
      fast
and the crowds grow thick splitting the tongue with
      trippers
and Dr. Fate comes and his nurse Miss Adjustable Parts
      with
a bag of revolutions called New Love War the throat hurts
there are fists growing up in the big parade to the end
you can feel the hands closing round in the downwind
      enterprise
mouth parched paino piano all twisted up inside in the
      other

then wake up with the morning you're clean lived
        through it's
over your shoulder Yesterday your old man's dream come
        true
your eyes fly back to their sockets you can see your voice
all the memorial in braille stretching back to that first big
shot of a shout out of the dark mouth who made you a
        lover.

                            1967

THE GARDEN

The fathers we run across, the brothers we need
and where's the woman holding the bag?
                    Over 49th street and Eighth Ave.,
it's like the sky opened up, she dropped the whole
thing here, my old man said over a dead
coffee. Raising eight-ouncers. His heart knitted
with *Hebrew-American*, the sperm people swimming
            outside
the championship movie of priests whores the navy
patentleather boos the platinum hair locked on
the arm of hooch. Rough crush and drubbing
inside. Hard combinations. The black father
came back with a short dig under my cheek, why
was I going away again?
        Blake fanatics on the corner. His tungsten
jabs broke against my nose turning red
Irish. I dug a couple cutting pities under his chin.
A wreck of an old shoe watched us through the window
drove a hard one right across the flynn of his moustache,
brought the elbows of his knees to the tabletop. It
looked finally like he was learning what he's taught.
Crowd yelled for kill. His head fell over, hair flowing

white and black like the letters of the book. I started
eating the stuffings of my mitts above him. When
I touched his hair my bandages burned to the skin:
He was the old man, what do you do with him?
A hundred magazines emptied *Love Romance & Time*.
Fritzie Zivic was playing four rounds of cheap ties
out of a valise at the entrance.

1967

EUROPE

You more powerful
than all the visions
You who died in fire
and Rainer's fragments
You who persist in me
as the distance here
Oh continent of Being
You awful old space
where I left my voice
where I saw my face
outside its member
You who keep in touch
day after darkness
You whom I cannot bear
You who drove me mad
with the old devices
You of the palpable
tenderness and real
depth uproaring night
You of impotence made
debonair with rage
made clear with limit

made free with loss
of all but the unending
compassionate weeping
that goes on under
the endless burning
the vivid hatred
the rich red love
the chthonic whole
the master's gong
the endless turning
back into time's
long bleeding friends
made into visible song.

1968

35

LONDON

The dignity of London lies deep with humiliations
	contained
The freedom of London resides in a simple blitzed
	courage
The power of London lives with a carefully conserved
	flame
The strength of London is the limitation of its Empire
The Empire of London is ruled at the high point by a
	queen
The ever-running blush of London is a Hampstead
	foxglove
The tweedy front of London hides the broken heart of a
	boy
The miniskirts of London are a feast for the untouchables
The hashish of London is only one of its many visions
The ladies of London are the last chattering style of
	Europe
The story of London is a bunch of snippets two and six a
	bunch
The university of London is no teacher and all class
The true underground of London is the tube
The tube is the intestine of a delicately passionate future

body which already contains the United States of the
Kidney

The United States of London wastes and spends for this
hunger but

The food of London is finer than the food of the United
States

The weather of London is the I Ching

The I Ching of London wears a beard or long hair and
when she walks by he is observed by everyone
touched by no one
and smiled at as if with that questioning accent that
goes up and up and up and never comes down.

1969

POINT LOBOS

The cypress tree, how long standing (just so
waiting to stop me so near
the Pacific below, that it should be
next to an old whaler's shack, throwing me

back in a flash: Other oceans, wanderers, O

I let missus and kids go on down the cove
after sealion cries wild
flowers. Her hair, the whole hard year
flapping lightly against her shoulders leading

them down, leaving me) just so

alone and face to face this cypress
tree that's said Stop
to mind and gut notions, and
I do so, in the way she for a whole summer

gone down now to the sea, who sees,

had not been able to get me, by any wile or
straightaway what a woman must do to,

and yet I do so obey, in the fall
of this night at highnoon, for the hell of

its dishevelled beauty:

The green, the deepgreen of windblown hair pasted back
and caught like that,
and the hieroglyph nuance of branches everywhere
bolted by sun and shadow, making a place

I want to enter in, under,

touch the trunk going up from the earth in a jet of,
then wonder of, muscle swinging
to the left a rivering eridanus, to
the right a solar candelabra

with form and number changing

with each turning step under, there are animals I've
never dreamed before
in sun or shadow, and the textures
of bark, I wonder

why red for a stretch here? what

brighter green hand ran the print of its palm down here?

blue bird screed thanks with what
quill of a tail? why
violet and yellow together?

or here where I bend

a whole flank washed clean by the sea air exposing
pink and white cells caught,
I could swear, stripped
to nucleus and protoplasm of naked eye

Myself

the torn elbows of the old grey rotting skin, messy
and half eaten-out pulp
with perfect little punctuations
woodpeckers make with their beaks

Myself

the scraped knees of a kid through the corduroy feel,
the spiderwork armpits,

the thousands of tiny cone-worlds at my feet
and the thousands still clinging

Myself

the tree I never see until I chop it out of me into a song
the children can ride the right river of
and she climb with wild flowers and love
to perch on my left arm, and smile, all

as the sun falls, a shutter, into the sea

1970

37

VENICE

There are a bunch of Mexican kids playing
baseball in the lot on Electric Avenue,
Venice. They have a tree, a slender
leafless poinsettia
for home's natural backstop,
ten or eleven kids and one girl
with breasts more mature than most of their heads.
But they run with life, all over the dirt,
and while they wait their turn
at the plate they sit on one of those
busted bright green convertible Buicks
sitting in the lot on two tires,
or hold the handlebars of their bicycles.

I thought I saw one swinging from a very old moustache.

You mustn't hold back the free play
of the countries that possess your blood.

They play it so that first base is third base
and why I should be thinking at that
of a hackie in Buenos Aires
turning to the customer in the back and talking

yiddish I don't know.

There goes, here comes a hard smash
over second base and through to
the outfield,
and here come six legs after it, which has just
rolled past me and across the Electric Avenue
gutter.

An old woman is pushing a lawnmower
on the sidewalk and turning into an alley,
her ass assuming the shape
of the cheeks of a Japanese master
of Zen.

A Black man coming out of the library
agrees with me fifty yards of eyes away:

there's something about letting a ball
roll has something to do with sunshine
America, and a longhaired postoffice
carrier likewise has stopped
pushing his leather bag

and is standing as if he were about to
raise his arm and drink everything

back to the beginning in raspberries,
licked blood, and that commune
of shouts at the top of the lungs
where no one listens and yet
every muscle hears
and is moved and sings.

1972

HEADLANDS

One went off to be
        alone by the great ocean
                voice

Another stood and sat
        at the same time

Another became myriad
        positions of meditation

Another descended the high
        rocks and entered
           the foam
     and ankle
        torrent

Another went off to be
        alone by the great
           ocean voice
hiding in a thicket

Another picked the nakedest
land's end flowers

Another turned into a
        heron

Another became a piece
           of driftwood

The one near the beginning
          of the poem
    became the wave
        and later was upon the earth

The heron became a
        whale which
   made us all throw
      up our arms

The positions of the yoga
        became the pollen
      eyes of the
  flower I picked for you

who were the center of
        the voice of the great
          ocean

as it came into our lives
       again

with the familiarity of
        every 'thing' in
            the world
its repeated crashing
            against the rocks
its drama and stillness
        of precipices
                and inlets
of erosions and incredible
        resuscitations
the clear foam spatter
        of the orgasms of
                the eternal voice
the origin of the
            electrical ether
now unstinging between
                us
the bees of scud
        wetly upon our
                faces
torrential freedom
        of the limbs
and the dreaming
        idioms
        of voyages

powerful as we floated
       on land which
          was the ocean
             itself
as human vessels
       of the horizoning
          of the letters
             of silence
long long longest
       spool of softness
in this fisherman's
       world
deep deep deepest
       sounding of
the life both whole
       and jettisoned
in instances of wave
       white
  foamed currents
  of the intangible
our throats our
       singing throats
  stilled in this
immensely
felt

inner mouth of
silence and
          turbulence
our deaths stilled
          at the point
               by the touch
of this long
life stretched out
before us like a fortune
told by rainbows.

1975
42

X L E B

From the top here
of Vesuvio's
I have just seen
a man with
spectacles
and a beard
come along
Adler's Alley
roughly
twenty-five years old
to the garbage bin and reach
in and lift
out a container
of pistachio
icecream
and lick it
with his fingers,
then reach in
for a piece of paper
and wipe his fingers
very delicately
and his mouth

very elegantly
and continue
on into the
mainstreet, what
can you
say to this
piece of bread ?
Dostoyevsky ?

1975

SOUL OF A PENCIL

With all the mustard of earthquake I say
to my bones, which tremble
indistinguishable from my bloodcells
after love, I say:
What has your mouth translated
                              tonight?

What skeleton of dust?
What totem rattle?
What homunculus uncial
      trapped in a vessel
scuttled for a kiss?
What pulverized muff tasting
of my own face in a whirlwind
of mapleleaves?
What norther than north,
      souther than south
      of this snatch of a poem?

I say, and I say, between
      uterine walls echoing my
      tonsils,

to the spool of umbilical
tape and the guts of my turban-wound brains,
I say to my shudders, to
     the savor of raw milk
left by your tongue
on my bicep,
     to the ghost of the ploughed
     fields of sex which irrigates
     my lines with blood weddings
     and shows me the worms
     in the earth of my very own flesh—:

Low clouds over the brims
     of straw hats dripping with
     sweat at the end of their
     bale day's work.

Wrists thick with veins
     bursting for the quench
     of the icecubes of nights
     of chance.
Across the flat chest of
     the middlewest of any-
     where etcetera
The tornado cut loose

from our bodies
    is doing the dance
that makes the trees run
    through the cornfields
and the telephone lines
    slither and snap
    and leave us discon-
    nected, looking at
    each other
with a gaze that grows
between us until it stops
and we step out of
the remains
of each other
as the sun comes up
between the bleeding
clench of our hands.

1975

A VILLAGE POEM

Albinoni's
Adagio for Strings always in me when
I step out into a North Beach
alley or street and see
the old Italian who walks
with two wooden sticks for canes,
his back humped over,
who must climb hill or level
fixed on sidewalk or gutter
as my eyes fix on his fate,
the sticks like ski-poles,
each step a climb,
in organ time,
with subtle variations, and how the
second swell of the orchestra
makes me throw open my voice
and sing accompaniment
to something lost and passional,
for the endurance of a wrinkle
that can't let go of its time,
and the way it is when
music kneads us like bread

because there's only wine,
a wooden table and the shoes
one has talked to since the Renaissance.

1976
4/3

BOOK

I return to the leaves
left in a poem I wrote
years ago in Paris
about Chevrenière-
sur-Marne, just outside
the city, how they fell
and heaped on the road
yellow and brown-speckled,
red-shot like bloodshot,
and blue and green
and rust. The moist
crushweight of footfall
through the small autumnal towns
of their trembling.
All the small
town leaves, the leavings
bunched, and myselves
in the hands of them,
in the provincial
prayer that ran beside
the river, muddy under
a grey and cloud-rolling

smokeweave of cigarettes
and chatter out of high
lapels. What a family
of fronds we were ! The
taste of us like the clear
prunelle of conversation.
Of streets, the uncut pages
of books. Leaves, loose again.
Folio after folio of tree.
And how we shed and shared
our skins to the small
watermark in time. *A-*
mer. America. So
big. But the leaf I return
to within, the face of
flight and transmigration,
simple and magically
carried by the stem
through the war towns,
through the thousand poems
when the tree was in rags
and rage—leaf like a
hand whole lands, by
visionary law, can fit into,
season and accent, inscape

of atoms threaded by
the river: I read your veins
and capillary trillions
like an allseeing blindman
brailling through his ecstasies.
Were you ever not leaf
to me, poem ? Poem to my
piecemeal, O leaf ?
From power to power
in the branching changes
of governments of breath,
your dance interwoven
through rhythms and dithyrambs,
the high seas of the siren
cries. And then a day
I sit all the way deep
in the still embryo of self.
And curve, translucently.
Does that sound alright ?
Shall we take this red
road of blood and wine-dropped
alliteratives ? Isn't the river
syllabling marvelously
through the scape ?
And I find you in almost

the same phrase
I left in the poem. The hand
of the leaf shape changed.
Samely. The town. The river.
The clouds very close
to the ground. Our
selves bunched
and nonetheless particled
out of the grammar
of the weather, a slow
sweet karma of
the already
gathering constellations
of the night in the leaves
between the covers and the spine.

1976

RUNNING POEM

I want to ride the prairie of your eyelids
like a pinto of kiss
and beat on the drum of a river
till its time gives way
and run like a small child with a squirrel for a head
and touch every wound into a poem
and remove the curse of Europe with a red philosophy
and wipe the curse of liquor from the mouth of the
      American dead
and open the pipe of a poem stuffed with cattail pollen
and look into the four corners of its eternity
and read the buckskin sky
chanting slowly under my breath
until you stand beside me saying: *Adobe, adobe!*
the way I used to lie in bed
when I was a child with a schoolroom for a head
whispering over and over: *Adobe, adobe!*
because you stood beside me as we worked to build it
you helped me like my mother
and all my poisons have made me forget your name

memory?

O dark one
O braid
O first, indian 1ove, O love of the people
I shall call you Running Poem
precisely because you're still so still
to feel you is to open the eyes of any jail
with a feather.

1976

VIMBA

Now we are going to take the land
by an undercurrent of music,
going to melt down the roots of ice
through immersions of dark hallelujahs.
We will wear our fool's gold
amuletic at the neck,
our twins, their doubles.
A polyglot of rhythm that in another life
was pain will walk the water it invents
every desert moment.
And I will quench my thirst
on your flowing shoulder,
sail with your rib canoes into the thicket.
Lush-green and big as a kid's smile,
the leaves will taste chicory-white
amid the plummeting brown suavities.
Everything will fall ascendingly in autumn
catching fire like bits from the paintbrush
of Hyppolite, celebrating the speckles of air.
And I will draw you on the floor of this ocean,
with sound as well as stroke of the breast
and thighway. The fish will be birds.

Everything will gill and swish again
but with a lovely, deeply charged innocence.
The child of five and the man of seventy
will be the same size as the trees and cities
will be carried in the palms like marbles.
I tell you water.
I tell you the un-suicided scuttle.
I tell you the underground underwater
where we fin and flicker, where landscape
is adoration and there is no end to the mango.
Your taste will be my smell,
my hearing your vision,
and everything bathed bronze
in the hydrogenic flood, on reefs where we
catch our breaths like scarves
painted the brightest colors of the sea,
wrap our bodies in savage tenderness,
spit out our hooks and worms with laughter
and never again be a bite
caught, yanked up dumb, smacked down whap
on a wet pier of slash, blood-smear, dying wriggle
and mere dead meat.

                                    1976

                        92

THE SACRIFICIAL LAMB

As I slept I heard
you call me in the voice
of our former life,
womanly, resonant, dark
eyelid of voice, voice with child,
voice of older passion, of
our lust and obscenities,
mimosa voice of vining power,
voice of blood and storm

And I went on sleeping,
I could no longer rise to that woman,
she had been wept away,
  many tissues at the bedside
  of a broken promise of wood,
  many tissues in the broken
  toilets of the hotel heart

She had arrived at you
called me in the voice of this life,
a girl's voice, a voice at once
  thin as a crik, as a hope like thread,

a fresh whisper of this new karma
    of love

I see your confusion clearly
and when I am wide awake
and kiss you,
I pass through the light
    water of the mask
and touch that dark ecstasy
          again,
who is silent who is otherwise
    wiser for the seachange,
who holds us both
    loving orphans of her thrall
    loving kisses of her continual
        rebirth
        gathered by our lips from
the scattered rags of air
    where she flung herself
one garment-demented day.

                  1976

"LET THE RAILSPLITTER AWAKE"

for Pablo Neruda

It was brown and white
it was on the rack
when I saw it first
when it opened my eyes
like the book that it was
on the rack
when it split the rails
of adolescent streets
when it called from
still further downtown
then I'd been,
down there with the masses
and mainstream
of the markets and pushed
carts and beggars,
it that was it which is IT:
the book on the rack,
the rack of the centuries'
inquisitional redemption,
Book now with a capital,

Book of elemental translation
of the earth's earth,
brown and white
　　　instant I saw opened it
　　　opened me,
so many comrades afterward,
so many letters within
　　　　　letters,
　　　human alphabets
　　　of the visionary
　　　　　arts,
reverberant to that moment
guitar burst like grapeskin,
diamonds became simple
crumbs of the bread
poems are shivered for,
the long two hemispheres
　　　of the body of a man's
　　　poems
broke from the pages
and began my inner
　　　hearing.

1976

WORKER'S POEM

You whose brows are knit
with electric streets, come sit beside
my fire-doomed face, you who gaze
on thin air, spaced out and longing
for nothing, broken violins
of bodies, diamonds of mind fractured
by the plague of money, come sit
in my winter flake, my room
which is part of this vast cage
where free birds break their wings
against the sunlight and warm
their suspicions at the broken
shoe-balance of the street.

1976

THE INTERNATIONAL HOTEL

When I finally ran through the cordon with the others
and reached the pickets, there was the sound
of sledgehammering. Into the mural on the Jackson St.
gallery wall, the cops were smashing into the Hotel's side.
And when the crowd jeered with rage at the desecration
of the mural I'd passed a thousand times and a thousand
        times
it had called me back to Chinatown and North Beach,
the cops called for reinforcements, goons with clubs
who stood guard along the smashed wall painted by
a collective of artists to honor their Asian-American
        heritage.

I still cry out, Down With Fascism! remembering Ray
staggering in the middle of the gutter after taking a club,
and those 75-year-old Chinese women and men walloped
as they pressed forward with us in sidewalk rage,
and that painted door splintered and ripped out of the
        mural's
landscape, leaving a wound I still dip my brushes in
these many years after, and write: LONG LIVE THE I
        HOTEL!

                                        1977

98

NICARAGUA

And where the dead heart
of an earthquake's anonymous buried
pulses, there too beats marimba.
And where the jungle leaves big as pamphlets
are turned by the winds of revolt,
there the tambor sounds
Nimbu Nimbu, clear water of the scoop hand
under the brim of sunlight,
and the *ollita* of the matrimony with revolution,
and the eyelid of *quijongo* is plucked
into a fervor of vision,
and now we here are there in the breath
of the *pito*,
a fifing from within the guts
of all the poem's martyrs;
a clear, thin but certain trill of compañeros:
Ernesto and Augusto, Roberto, Rigoberto,
Alejandro, Pancho, Luis, Vladimiro —
with the roots of murdered women and children erupting
from our mouths like *Nyayu Nyayu* masks
of the deep thicket dance,
the deadly serious dance of the american earth

turning turning in its intestines,
burning with hope for the people of umber
and wound, emanating from the plexus center,
the epicenter of mud, disease and hunger
with a moan so seismic
the belly of greed will sunder
and all the swallowed villages
will separate themselves
from the vomit and the swill
and blossom red tomorrows
around the lakes of simple water.

1979

DOPE

You toke and then talk
to me but as you talk
your toke is saying
Me, Me, Me,
is fixing me to your
I, I, I,
so that we're really not
listening to each other,
really not receiving
each other's words
but rather taking place
before one another
as images.
And because that
Me, Me, Me
is rooted in the pain
that made you
toke in the first place,
the pain that's in us all
in this hell of a hearse
of euphoria called
the U.S.A.,

which keeps us
in a playpen
flinging our things
every-which-way,
eating our shit,
banging our toys
against the bars, crying
Me, Me, Me,
it's important to know:
dope IS that shit
and you only contribute
to nothing when
you're on it,
and nothing's
so utterly boring,
get off it
and see for yourself
what the world is like
without you.

1981

NY, NY

It's big
It's ugly
I hate it
I love it
I'm free
O
Talk to me
Can't you hear me
I can't leave it
I'll do anything for it
It's so big
It's filthy
It's so sweet
I adore it
I'm staying
I'll never leave
It's in me
It's so cruel
I hate it
I love it
It's mine
I own it

It's mine
Again and again
I say I hate war
I love it
It's disgusting
It's awesome
I love it
I won't go
I promise
It's beautiful
Talk to me
Can't you hear
Me loving
O it's so brutal
It's so shit
Talk to me
Tell me
What I should do
Anything
It's marvellous
I'll never stop
Loving it
Never never
Never never
Never.

1983
50

VLADIMIR MAYAKOVSKY

You, thunderer and swirl of
       the flag of blood and roses,
kneader of the bread of poem,
deathless comrade of dithyramb
   and liberty,
you whose suicided life
   I carry as a forge,
who first strode the street
   of this century,
ai, you were the first
singing through the slum of trash
and the molecules chained
to a thousand yesterdays,
wiper of the gravy of history
from the mouth of obese lies,
servant of revolution,
you who, among men, stormed
the pallid lips of neutrality
and apathy,
not as a stud of craven doom,
not as *semblable*
but as a thrust and momentum

of mass and energy
announcing the towering totems
of humanity freed from the hut,
you russian more american
than english,
you sabbath-destroyer
and leveller of twirpery
and religious doubletalk,
I have plucked the bullet
so many times from your brain
I could feed a hundred
armed struggles with your dream.

1983

ONE NIGHT

One night, many North Beach years ago,
after a reading at the old Coffee Gallery,
drunk, I found myself in my single bed
at the old New Riviera hotel
making love to a young woman.
She was fair and lithe and craving
and I was lonely and poet-stung.
After love she slept in my arms.
It was then I saw her body's marks, the extensive
track record of her race
and rose and sat and wrote
a dozen little love poems
to her beauty and despair,
and all you can imagine as she slept.
She was gone by morning
but I saw her two weeks later
on one of the Columbus Day floats
that passed down Stockton by the Park.
She was among the thin women
celebrating America's founding
and she waved the friendliest pale hand
and smiled the warmest faint smile.

I never saw her again.
I don't remember her name when sober.
I don't remember it when drunk.
It's like the many names
I remember then don't remember
from rock and roll to punk.
She was a young American woman.
We'd had a one-night stand,
many North Beach years ago.
No more Vietnams.

1984

SPIRALS

Onward and upward,
the smoke from the chimneys
spirals,

spirals even today.
A generation and more
of clouds
made of Communists, Catholics
Jews, Gypsies, Witnesses,
Gays.

Jet planes fly through
them. They
are all over the world,

rising and devǫloping,
joined with the burned
of El Salvador, the Hiroshima scorched,
the roasted starving
of Africa,
the diaspora
of Palestine in flames.

You smoke them, your
toke is them, we
blow the dead
away into air.

A Black man
is tied to a tree
in Georgia and burned
to ash. 1893.
It spirals even today.

You will never
escape them,
they
arise
and develop,
invincibly.

Deny them
and try breathing.

They will haunt
you to the end
of your
sperm and your
egg.

In the
last
gasp
of the
molecule
they'll
arise.

1984

51

MOTHER

We are not in this world
a long time ago
it happened it was over:
the world the war the world war.
I took you by the hand
through it,
tiniest hand, tiniest star.
You didn't move then
I was dead, then you were dead.
In the open mouth of grief
there is a candle.

I am not with my breath,
I am the slow peeling away
of the skin
and all that all the deaths
I've seen registers
in my eyes.
I have been a laughing tree
beside a stove
of honeyed bananas,
I have been a silver fox

and the elegance of heels,
I have been what has
brought you down
and the words you look up,
I have been the spit-upon
and the ganged,
the slain and the invincible,
the bitch of moons,
the whiplash of compassion
behind the drug of sluts,
the red thread that
liberates all convicts,
the thimble that balances
your jiggers,
the kalimba that wraps
your nightmares in lullabies,
the power of birth
when a child dies.

We are not in this world
a long time ago
it happened it was over:
the world the war the world war.
I took you by the hand
through it,

tiniest hand, tiniest star.
Why should I weep now now
that you have entered the darkness?
Many like me are around you.
Our ether is without end.
Should we never speak again,
you shall write our conversation.
Should my voice fall short of your heart
(but that is impossible,
you're still such a child,
I'm weeping at a window),
other voices will lift mine
and carry it to the center
of your breathing.

O my beloved, when you burst into flames,
when your bones were blistered,
at those precise moments,
who drove the seeds in a rapid
torrent of thighs and targeted
the yearning eggs with glory?
When you grew like a primer
into a text of rage
at all the injustice of this
profiteering hell,

114

when your mind was broken,
when your sex was split
like Korea, Vietnam,
like the North and South,
when poisons came with pleasure
and the antidote was dead,
who cut through the air
as if wringing a chicken's neck?
who tore the feathers and flung them
to cushion your fall?

I am the creature who runs through the streets
screaming your name against the mockery,
I am the sleep of the suicide
and the cataract of immemorial hair,
I am the attack of liberty on the hard of heart
and the poem on the hard of hearing.
The solitude, the grace, the smile
that returns your smile
from the depths of the biology
of a labor and joy
only the heartbeats of the dithyramb approach,
only the soul thrums of the cosmos define.

We are not in this world
a long time ago
it happened it was over:
the world the war the world war.
I took you by the hand
through it,
tiniest hand, tiniest star.

1984

GARDENIA

That woman walking talking to herself
in furs.
And that one in the doorway smelling
of cardboard and rags, mumbling.
And that man, drunk, babbling on the sidewalk,
Chinese, holding a pink plastic bag.
And that man, sober, talking to a lampost,
and that young hooker in front of the hotel,
smelling of dead orgasms,
venereal acne broken out on her face,
whispering to herself with a sullen
rat of lip:

dislocated, deranged, dissident, atonal,
joyless, loveless, timewarped,
space-killed,
eaten by the worms of money,
bitten-away faces, loneliness handouts,
pitiful claptrap dimes,

—over the ear of Socialism
they are petals of the most fragrant gardenia
and every single one of their syllables is heard.

1985

Sitting against a treetrunk in Dolores Park
amid the Chilean solidarity gathering,
my eyes beheld three tiny daisies
in the grass, their little pollen hearts
attacked by flies. Nearby, yellowjackets
were flying over a jungle of blades
of grass and brilliantly green-backed
horseflies were making merry on
a flute of dogshit. I had lowered
my eyes from the speeches, and even
the People's Tribune was stacked at
my side. So much movement
in nature! A butterfly alighted on
the front page and walked along
the headline as if reading it. The
flies went on eating the hearts out.
The horseflies were absolutely drunken
on the excrement. The yellowjackets
were strafing and landing and
taking off again. It was the guerrilla
war, it was *mir*, it was peace. So much
movement, so much space in an inch. This
Neruda earth.

1985

HAITI

One day in the future these sounds are seeds of,
there will be a moment when not even the monkeys chirp
        in the trees,
when burros will hold their brays,
when the coconut-milky clouds will not stir in the sky,
when the thatchwork of huts will not be gossiping
and there is no breeze or sweat between your body and
        your rags
One day when that moment lived for years, for centuries,
        is here
and everything is still
like death
or zombie bread holding its breath,
a drum will begin sounding
and then another and another, multiplying,
and the voices of the simidors will be heard in every field.
And the backs,
those backs with everything written on them,
which have bent like nails hammered into the wooden
        cross
of the land for ages,
will plunge their arms into the ground

and pull out the weapons they've planted.
For the drums aren't an invitation to a voodoo ceremony.
The voices of the simidors are singing another song.
The lambis are growling lions of Africa.
And it isn't the cranium of a horse hung on the wooden
         cross
braided with limes;
it isn't a wooden cross at all that's planted in the good
         earth
of new Haiti.

On the night of that day the taste of a mango will be
a rapturous fireworks bursting and dying into
the ecstasy of the simple truth in our mouths.
Our acres will sleep with their arms round each other.
The child freed from terror and death will bound with
the boundless, and the maize amaze the sky upon waking
for as long as humanity is.

1985

EZRA DOG

I

Did you say Ezra

                Dog?

I did.

Do you mean Ezra, the dog of the beautiful

Filipino woman who lives on the Beach?

I do not. I mean Ezra Dog

Pound. And his kennel

of little whelps.

Who bark about what a great poet

Ezra Dog was, and is,

even though his politics was bad,

who apologize for his wet black

bows to the gunmen of Europe,

for his wet black bowwows

while patrols sweep wetbacks

into the corrals of Texas,

stuff them into trucks

the way the gunmen did the Jews

while Ezra Dog down the road

was whining on Italian

radio about the halfbreeds of Europe,
about the gorillas of America,
those Jews, and those Blacks
being lynched by plantation folk
with pitches of voice in the crux
no different than dead dog Ezra's.
And now that Ezra's republican
eco eco economic
fascism's written on everybody's brow,
and that sell-out's liberty
and the sell-out liberties
of this yipyip-hooray American
experiment

has the universities of the nation
churning out those wagtag
little foams and grovels of capitalism,
and even the broad lap
of the Zionism he denounced,
in sadistic benignity
with Buddha, Confucius, and Tao (Jones),
lets his image lie across it
like a mongrel pieta,

I'm goin' down to the dock
and see that Dog, the shepherd of Germany,

gets the hell out of San Francisco and
back to South Africa
with its cargo of rabies.

II

And, and I use the word
advisedly,
when Dog was kenneled in St. Elizabeth's,
defended by literateurs
and young snipperwhaps
in rebellion against the family
grey matter of desolation
after the Bomb,
"in Italy" he told Charles Olson,
"I was always a Stalinite,
never a Trotskyist."

Can you beat that
mutt?!

Who'd barked against bolsheviks
throughout the thirties and forties,
whose cantos are
usury's imperialist

invasion of arrogance's images
on workingclass senses,
and who would take up
with the racist John Casper,
even while in the sickhouse,
and scribble jingo gibberish
for his southern hatesheet.

All the while being apologized for
by cold-war saps of technique,
honored by Bollingen
stuffed stiffs,
even proto-beatniks,
for his contribution to American letters,
his breaking of new ground,
his imagistic elegance,
his translative prowess.
In the new age of power through
schizophrenia,
in the loose corners of the mouth
of marijuana,
in the new cycle, the immigration
of the corporate state,
the fascist's sell-out experimentalism
would be evoked and re-evoked

until, lo and behold,
universities and writing cliques
were glutted
with Dog's disciples:
packs of America's finest
writing hounds
all pardoned,
like himself,
for writing well,
according to the book (the bankbook)
by the hicks of hell.

J. my name is Jack
and my woman's name is Sarah.
We come from San Francisco
and we don't sell the people.

1986

THE UNNAMEABLE

There is a word
for the unobstructed bliss
after loving,
the waking sleep that is quick
with poem,
the clarity the other side of the taste
of drink and nicotine
or latakia,

the smells of everywhere
invading with fragrance—

O simple sleep of the sitar
of body,
I play you with my eyelashes
the way the feelers
of a cockroach
write its brown verse
to a breadcrumb in the pantry.
It is a time when
everything is put together
like the thumb and the forefinger.

The sun is being born
from the egg in the moon
of your hips;
it will take all night, my sperm,
these shards along the sea,
your dreams, and then
it will belong to the rest
of the world again.

I do not know the word in this tongue
for this interlude between
your body and the plunge
of my own into sleep,
but never is my poem
more poem,
never is stillness
so ripe.
I am like the word *uva*
or *undinal,* this very action
of writing ferments me,
I do not fall but burst
asleep beside you
as if I were drunken ink
rounded by a grapeskin
sharira

your tender gestures
forever blot
into indelible tones.

1987

HOME

(to the National Union of the Homeless)

Winter has come.
In doorways, in alleys, at the top
of churchsteps,
under cardboard, under rag-blankets
or, if lucky, in plastic sacks,
after another day of humiliation,
sleeping,
freezing,
isolated, divided, penniless,
jobless, wheezing, dirty
skin wrapped around cold bones,
that's us, that's us in the USA,
hard concrete, cold pillow,
where fire? where drink?
damned stiffs in a drawer
soon if, and who cares?
shudders so familiar to us,
shivers so intimate,
our hands finally closed in clench
after another day panhandling, tongues

hanging out;

dogs ate more today, are curled

at the feet of beds, can belch, fart,

have hospitals they can be taken to,

they'll come out of houses and sniff

us dead one day,

pieces of shit lying scattered here

in an American city

renowned for its food and culture.

The concrete is our sweat hardened,

the bridge our vampirized blood;

the downtown, Tenderloin and Broadway

      lights—our corpuscles transformed

      into ads;

our pulse-beat the sound *tengtengendeng*

of coins piling up on counters, in

phonebooths, Bart machines, *tengtengendeng*

in parking meters, pinball contraptions,

public lavatories, toll booths;

our skin converted into dollar bills,

plastic cards, banknotes, lampshades

for executive offices, newspapers,

toiletpaper;

our heart—the bloody organ the State

gobbles like a geek in a sideshow
that's become a national circus of the damned.

O murderous system of munitions and inhuman rights
that has plundered our pockets and dignity,
O enterprise of crime that calls us criminals,
terrorism that cries we are fearful,
greed that evicts us from the places we ourselves
      have built,
miserable war-mongery that sentences us to misery and
        public exposure as public nuisances to keep a
        filthy republic clean—
this time we shall not be disappeared
      in innercity ghetto barrio or morgue,
this time our numbers are growing into battalions
      of united cries:

We want the empty offices collecting dust!
We want the movie houses from midnite till dawn!
We want the churches opened 24 gods a day!
We built them. They're ours. We want them!
No more doorways, garbage-pail alleys,
no more automobile graveyards,
underground sewer slums.
We want public housing!

No more rat-pit tubing, burnt-out rubble-caves,
no more rain-soaked dirt in the mouth,
empty dumpster nightmares of avalanches of trash
        and broken bricks,
screams ot women hallucinating at Muni entrance
        gates,
no more kids wilh death-rattling teeth under
        discarded tarp.
We want public housing!
we the veterans of your insane wars,
workers battered into jobless oblivion,
the factory young: fingers crushed into handout
        on Chumpchange St.,
the factory old: spat-out phlegm from the sick
        corporate chest of Profits.
Instead of raped respect, jobs
with enough to live on!
Instead of exile and eviction in this,
our home, our land,
Homeland once and for all
for one and all
and not just this one-legged cry
on a crutch on a rainy sidewalk.

1987

54

132

THE NIGHT

for Cornelius Cardew, People's Composer

There is a night that does not fall
when the sun dies,
that does not belong to the clock
yet is worn
like an invisible armband of a
millennial moment.
A child is born and wears it,
no matter he suckles in joy
or wails at a starving dug.
There is a night-music burned
into the soul of every atom,
a music that belongs to the motion
of that endless night
so excruciating in its truth,
so elemental in its resonance
of dissonant despair,
it is rarely performed,
it is unbearable with grief;
its skizzenbooks lie in boxes
in cellars or attics of houses

where people listen to sounds
of popular liberation, musics
that carry them from one
copacetic joy to the next
through their days.

Sometimes this other music
will manage to find its way out
of a darkness that amounts to subversion:
a record will be made, a concert performed;
it will rise and present itself
as the night that underlies
all the nights so desperate for breath,
sounds are made to fill up every hole
so that this other music, this other
night, not be sounded.
Sometimes it is; sometimes it finds,
through a crack in the headlong
rush of survival,
a solitude that calls it forth,
a conjunction of sorrows that needs it
and would knead it by means of
the fluttering hands of their hearts
into a bread that really is present.
Then we can hear it emerging

with fingers scraping
on the ceilings of our own screaming, gagging mouths,
with rifle-butts on brains and raisin-eyes floating
in sockets of blood,
with riddles of bullets down the back of a child,
with the sounds of ankles being broken,
with the crackles of immolation
and the winebottle of gasoline drunk
by a collapsing wall.
It emerges, it brings the perennial of darkness
close to our nostrils.
We smell that night of death, which triumphed and died,
and the time it will take
to die of it:
the rest of our lives.

1989

JULY 4th EVE 1990 (< Signs for me)

Walking along downtown Geary St.
after a town hall meeting
on censorship in the arts,
we stopped to give some money
to a mother holding her sleeping baby
as she squatted, shivering,
at an empty theater entrance.

Next door, *Les Miserables* had
an hour earlier closed its doors
on the last of its audience.
And a couple of shops along,
in the window of an art gallery,
Joseph Stalin was embracing
Marilyn Monroe,

he smiling in his grey braided
generalissimo jacket,
she posing as if the painter
had been a camera and the world.
The birthday of our independence
was just a half an hour away
as we walked through San Francisco.

1990

136

It was a happy day
when he was born
34 years ago
my blond son.

How golden the sun
in the park today,
how happy the birds
and flying balls.

I sit in golden light
almost forgetting
he's eight years gone
because the sun

is so like his hair
and the air like
the golden laughter
of his love.

Eight years old and
into a radiant windup.
Here comes a perfect
strike of light

upon an old old glove.

1990

NELLIE

After his shouts, the strops, her screams, the thrown things,
the doorslam, the bitter weeping,
out of the thin box, as the delicate paper was parted,
she'd lift the sheer mojud stockings
and run her fingertips along them,
slowly smiling girlishly again.

She'd begin singing a Perry Como song,
she loved Perry Como and would sing
the same song he sang, all day long,
on the Make-Believe Ballroom Time.

Then, in a black brassiere strapped to her freckled
        shoulders,
she'd sit on the bed, fit the stockings,
stand up and notch them to the garters
that hung down from her black girdle.
A ripple of fat ran round her waist, squeezed out
by the girdle, different from
the plumps that swelled out from her brassiere.
And I saw a blue bruise, the shadow
of a belt-buckle on her thigh.

But she was singing again, and over the girdle
she'd put on a pair of pink bloomers,
and over everything, then, a brown-and-white flowerprint
summer-golden dress.

Her white heels had holes in the toes where her nail-polish
showed through. The bottle of polish, tweezers, lipstick,
rouge, brush and emeryboard were on the vanity table
over there looking in the mirror.

Her lips swam in the Como song with rose-red strokes,
reaching the end with a shiny glow,
like the waxy cameo of her mother
on the brooch in the drawer.

She'd hold out her hand and say, "Come, darling . . ."

We'd walk hand in hand up and down our street
                    in the twilight,
and the neighbors would cry out: "Hi, Nellie!" or "Hello,
Mrs. Hirschman" and "Hi, Jackie. My, how you've grown!"

1990

HUMAN INTERLUDE

for Terry Garvin

She was standing against
      the wall near
the Tevere Hotel holding
      a plastic cup
as it began to rain.

I dug for a coin, walked
      up to her
and dropped it in.
      It fell to the bottom
of an orange drink.

I blushed, looked into her
      ravaged eyes and skin
          and hair prematurely
greying, and said
I was sorry, I'd thought

she needed some bread.
      "I do," she said
and smiled, "I was

140

just having a little
drink."

And we stood there
      laughing together
as we watched the raindrops fall
      on the orange lake
above the drowning money.

1990

IN MEMORIAM
RAY THOMPSON (1943–1990) 46

Of the streets,
of begging hands and windblown cardboard,
of flophouse doorways or the lot behind the autobody
        shop,
of evictions from one downpour to another
and the trembling coffee,
the burning corner can,
the scavenged alleys,
the scratched and ravaged graffiti,
the transient handbills
and collectives of alone,

he was a poet
who wrote the deep lines the rotting weather
of this system cuts into human faces,
who saw in the cracks and the fissures
endurance birthing flashes of a radiant
lava-whirl of erupting rage,
and how hungry hunger is for it!
how widespread homelessness is for it!
how fertile futility is for it!

in this land where every living being or thing
is up for grabs or sale,
how headlong suffering is for it!

Earth, be mended
in the tears
of your seams, O ragged Earth,
be healed in your desire
for his body
through these tears. Mix him
with the thunders you've stored,
and with the rains,
the suns, the lightning-cracks
and the strokes of your loving zodiac
wrap him home, wound in his friends'
never-ending memory of his ascendings.

1990

143

JESSE

Keep me away from that bitch, he said, I mean
the priest came outta the church and she
pulled down her pants and pissed
right in front of him (the same padre
who slammed his doors on the foodline
on Good Friday two years ago),
and all night on the sidewalk in front
of the restaurant down there she was fuckin'
some guy, that bitch's in-
sane!

And he smiled half-terrified and put a brown five down
        on my upcoming palm.

Was Jesse. Is.
A raving equine beauty
with chestnut-blond hair,
strong horse-teeth,
in dirtywhite pants, cowboy boots,
pushing a shoppingcart from Saroyan Alley up to the
        church steps
two blocks away, and then back down, or these days

144

pulling a straw square basket with a leather leash
        attached
and a bag, her leather jacket, and yellow blanket folded
        inside.

Sleeps with this one in the Alley,
that one in a doorway,
that one at the top of the steps
of St. Francis of Assissi,
panhandles the day for wine food cigarets,
and if you approach her her eyes go wild,
crazed-animal, caged-animal wild,
and if you touch her her clench her bite
hard down inside, the zing of fear
and violence, love's
a tooth her whole body
a fang impacted with thunder-rot,
who know what else, and

drive! she, who pushes
or pulls, is
down on her butt between the men on a broken step
or in sidewalk sprawl, swigging laughing yelling:

"The pigs they're ignorant"

Or up and haywire: "What a beautiful motorcycle
you have. Got any spare change?"

Or writing graffiti on the Alley wall.

Or hunched up in a doorway hugging a bottle
of wine to her chest, crowing, "When
O when am I gonna get to the USA?"

1990

TO JULIAN BECK

In a time when
theater was made into an obsolete entertainment by
            television,
you led a band of naked cries
onto the boards of a nation up to its teeth in death,
organized a company against that death,
pulling up the rotten bourgeoisie,
driving even the anarchists of everything, from art and hash
and the no-government-but-love's-pacific
slash of theatric clarity,
to collective distraction.
I was one
who caught the thrust of your direction in the guts,
translated the cries of that junk-mad polemicist
who godded over your company with his lucid deleriums.
I knew you
as a shining force in the midst of decay, your troupe
the only subversive ensemble in American theater
for a generation.
May its courage, in the long nights of the people's
            struggles ahead,
always be with us, with your wild eloquence.

At the moment you expired,
a red star flew to the black flag of anarchy
and blazoned itself on it
with your five arms.

1991

THE OLD WOMAN

Bus driver and I understand
that little old woman
can hardly stand;
so next time you're at
the mouth of a bus,
lend a hand.
Even your momma's a
child near the end.

1991

DANCING DAVE:
IN MEMORIAM DAVID BRONK, POET

Dancing Dave, all of 35, is dead.
He won't come back from
a blue odee this time,
or gently put a finger to
his lips as his blond gangly form
floats along these streets and alleys,
or fire one-liner non-sequiturs
that always seem to fit into
the synchrony of these insane times,
or publish a poem of sensitive brilliance
in the journal between the ears.

Louie, the barker in front
of the girlie palace, says,
of all the dopers he's known
Dave was the gentlest,
never came on heavy from underneath,
always floated as if on LSD.
And Taura, who works in the Caffè Trieste,
bursts into tears in both
American and Portuguese,

knowing his eyes won't be
zooming in on the markings
on a ladybug's eggs anymore
down on a leaf in the park.

1991

ON A LINE BY WHITMAN

Suddenly there are no dead I want to remember
and my good love isn't desperate for a poem.
I'm beside myself with calm, stretched out
in my hotel room in San Francisco.
What must be done, the revolt in my pen,
has surrendered to this quiet
musing on nothing in particular.
The world's whizzing and whirling outside
but I'm more inclined to the hairs on my chest.
They've been there forty years or more
hardly noticed with so much to do,
and now they're turning grey.
Suddenly I feel I've missed them,
their red youth, the darkening way they attracted
many kisses to the flesh that lay beneath them.
I've really paid them little mind, let alone senses,
and now they'll soon be white, and what can I say?
That they didn't belong to me?
That they didn't mean very much?
When it comes to the body's poor old road,
every one must be a touch.

1991

WHEN WE TEAR TOMORROW OPEN

for Sarah Menefee

When there aren't enough pencils to go 'round,
a teacher's forced to pay for them out of her pocket,
she has children, they need
to write.

A mother's relieved in quotes of her hungry kids
and put into the slammer for defrauding in quotes
welfare of 130 bux.

No wonder, so easily, the teenager's "I'm outta here!"
and meaning a lethal hotshot in the arm or a swing
over the rail of the (Golden) Gate: sheer plod does *not*
make sillion shine, just a leftover tinfoiled sandwich
in a garbage bin.

"Kafka wrote this building," Keith McHenry said
standing in the marble corridor of 850 Bryant awaiting
the trial of Sarah Menefee for having given free food
"without a permit."

And Jackson smashed by the cops into a window

153

and King savaged by bats held by men in blue sheets
in the gutter.

The glass the cuts
the bruises the cuts
the indignities and still
the collateral cuts
and more coming
and more . . .

What the hell are we in this for?
Our good name?
The system's already numbered it.
Our dying shmatas? — worthlessness, a m nags
Our clear thoughts about the end of western civilization?
Your hopeless feud with the devil?
My foot?

I want some breakneck speed to wrap me 'round
in a typhoon of people's rights.
No more half-assed splinter-routes to a trickledown reform.
No more gunpowder idea without feet in the real.

I'm talking about yesterday's calamity and how the law
comes down with its teeth closing out the story.
Gets in the way of the future.

Upholds its relation to property.
Leaves its scars on every soul.
A ticket, a warrant, an injunction, the sweep of its
foolish liberty. To be a cellular phone
to a corporation.

Alright, getting this off raw, without much to swing on.
The lights *are* going out in the west.
The whole pack's slivered into insidiously
                              shepherded individuals,
chopped into instances, cyclical What's up? Hi there!
and other one-liney spots.

Hopeless stuff, crackbrained
liberty. Nothing fits right
foot and the left is
dead.

We'd better organize and fight together and put some real
class in that anarchy it's fitted us all out with,
because you can virtually smell the clanking
military might right in your neighborhood.

When we struggle together,
from the very first ascent,
the lash will be stayed, the club paralyzed in the air.

And when we go deeper together,
deeper than sex or race, deeper than the ancestral
faces of the dead with their souls of blood
and the tenderness that curls clear down
in the spiral of the genes,

when we tear tomorrow open
and all together now throw our lives into our voice
and our voices into the song,

it cannot hold us back,
it must give way (it's already crumbling
                           of its own exploitations),

we can't but be
what all this human injustice
was meant to be toppled by,

and it will be,
we know it will,
we who have mastered
the smithereens.

1991

DAY OF THE DEAD

for Queen Trancila

The woman, as I walked by,
who all year long drifting and bundled in dirty
heavy clothes and carrying a sack of godknowswhat
on her back, on top of which a beautiful
cat with a collar and leash-rope sat as she walked,
which died or got lost a month or so ago,
and who always never smiled
and in her passing eyes looked
enduringly mad and ragpickingly alone
now is down on the Portsmouth Square
grass-ledge above the moonsplashed sidewalk
wallowing with kisses in the neck of a guy
she's found on the way
and going at his skull as if it were made of sugar
on this Day of the Dead night which is
home to all homeless lovers.

1992

THE CROWBAR SONG

And on the dead homeless,
and the dead homes with the living homeless in them,
capitalism shines its dirty moonlight, its rotten smug glow,
so give us some moonshine to chug-a-lug, and a whiskey
      a-go-go.

The dead in the streets
have been numbered again, and the number's beyond last
      year's,
and that's not counting those suiciding allover. All over,
      over here.
So give us some whiskey to chug-a-lug, and a moonshine
      a-go-go.

I'd like to hear the sound of the pry, of the pried-open
      splinters,
of the rip-tooth scream, of the screech of the boards
      being torn
from the stone of the lock-out building itself, and the hole
      born,
the hole the homeless pour through so they not be dead
      on arrival.

Gimme that crowbar, where's the next prison we liberate
for the street?
I wanna pull with the rest of us till we hear that wood
give birth.
And the long umbilical of homeless men and women of
good earth
find a bit of womb in the night. Clean moonglow. Hugs
of solidarity.

1992

REQUIEM FOR THE WAR DEAD

We will not know, we've been told, who they are,
the sons and daughters of the working class.
Strewn across the sands, they'll be
gathered, labelled, bagged and flown
to a twilight hangar in Delaware.

Gracie Beavers
Shawn Bermingham
Christopher Berry
Jimmy Burks
William Butters
Donna Conklin
Warren Dillard
Peter De Dolce
Stephen De Dolce
Charles Fountain
Danny Hitchcock
Stephen Richard Legro
Rutherford Loneman
Anthony Lopez
Bruce Martin
John Wesley More

Roxanna Peters
Susan Jan Reddy
Chena Risley
William Socia
Howard Stansell
Ray Thompson

They could be the above, who died
in attacks on the heart,
winter-whipped to death,
debris found at the bottom of flights
of stairs in TL hotels,
hit and run-overs,
slumped frozen panhandlers,
lesionaires of AIDS
drilled by hypothermia under cardboard
or in abandoned cars,
riddled with pneumonia,
barraged by waves till drowned
in a beach dug-out,
battered for a swig or some change,
lung-arrested
brain-arrested,
heart-arrested
and iced.

Might as well be the above;
for all we know,
they are the above,
and below—
                    a potter's field
of an arlington
growing and growing
the no-one's rose
of the wars' homeless.

1992

59

WILDEBEEST

You said, as we watched
an animal being born in Africa,
isn't it wonderful that one creature
literally comes out of the body
of another?

About a month later
I thought:
And enters the body of the world,
grows into living prime,
then goes toward death and dies,
leaving the world's body.

About a month later I heard:
Enters the womb of death,
so, you see, it just goes on and on,
entrances, entrancings and exits
that are themselves new entrances.

Who said that? I cried.
The voice of matter, which really never dies,
I heard as I tumbled out of my mother.
She was happy to see another
wildebeest outside. And so, I suppose, was I.

1992

163

*"I will not descend among
professors and capitalists"*
—*Walt Whitman*

I was leaning against a desktop
publishing store window
on Sacramento St., waiting
for the #1 bus to take me
over the hill, reading
"Among the blacks. . ." from OLSON Magazine
when a "Whattaya readin', white man. . . ?"
jerked my eyes up to see
a not-black not-white
guy with his buddy (who continued
up the hill), holding a can
of beer in a paper bag, —
Filipino, I thought, at first.

"A book of poems," I said directly.

"Can you read me one?" he sloshed
sincerely enough.

I recited one of my own by heart:

I know bellies,
children's bellies
big with nothing
pregnant hunger.

Inside of them,
empty mouths
crying: Why?!
crying: When?!

No more lies.
No more pies
in the sky.
Organizing

from the guts,
from the poor up
can be done
must be done

will be done.
Had enough?
Off your duff.
Let's make Revolution.

His eyes widened, clarity coming through,
"Hey, that's good," he said. "I'm
with you," so I gave him a People's Tribune
as he was starting after his friend.

Continued reading Olson's poems (left out Charles
of the body of his work) about a Black
murdered by 25 white men because of
his voice, when

the not-Filipino, actually
as it turned out, but—coming back down—
Hawaiian named Rick (he said,
and he'd looked at the paper
and could he write to it ("of course,"—)
and this was his buddy, Juan,
with a gothic Detroit "D"
on his baseball cap, ("Your home town?")
No, he was from Sanantone,

they just came back down to see
did I need, was everything okay, did I
need some money,—No, I was
okayfine. See you, brother. Have a good one.

They went back up the dark hill
to the Chinatown Moon Festival.
Hope they'd be alright.

Had the sense
I just was in
a genuine American
poetic experience.

Wanted you
to know it.

1993

VARIATION ON A SPIRITUAL

Steal away, steal away
anything you can
get your hands on
in the ol' Safeway.

Times just ain't what
they seem, they're worse
than a backseat ride
in a Cadillac hearse.

That guy in white's
grown a pair of tits
walking down the aisle
of kibbles and bits.

Well, in this 'hood
an ol' transvestite's
nothin' very special
round midnight.

Steal away, steal away
anything you can
get your hands on
in the ol' Safeway.

1994

IRISH BROGUE

for Sean Jackson

If it were less than a river rushing through fingers
of the harp played daily and, at the elbow, the piping
of the current,

or more than a mountain of a dream among the cairned
humps of bellies all stouted and open to the sun full
of song,

if it were less than a struggle stretched to the breaking
pints of victory on the bars of the jail of centuries
of lies,

if it were less black where it's green and less red
where its blood furies over the empty purses dangling
from women's arms, the empty days in the eyes of hungry
       heads,

it wouldn't be brogue, it wouldn't be the spiral turn
in the road of the human tongue's journey to light,
it wouldn't be

the end of night and the mourning for Ireland done,
and the spawn of morning-glories upstreaming.

1995

ON THE DEATH OF WILLEM DE
KOONING, AMERICAN PAINTER

When I think of the victories
we must win,
whether here for the workers and the poor
or everywhere against police brutality,
that is, throughout the world of
the New Class and the massing
of its energies for the global struggle
against the global thugs and their
cancerous world-state corps,

when the really generous expansion
from within revolution's process
simply takes held of the heart
and lifts it like an Albanian
unlocking the doors to the jails,
or Willem DeKooning raising that giant
brush of his *Bolton's Landing*,
that giant moustache of a brush

like what janitors use to paint
the floors of the world the color
of human labor, then I know

that monumentality of feeling at one
with what's heroically simple and real
as an answer to Death, and I can
re-begin belonging to the dream
of humanity again.

1995
62

XILOTL

Xihualhuian olloque yaoyoaque ~
Come forward, O ballplayers, warriors
you of the rubber and the marigold.
I am the skeleton of chocolate
inside the skin of the Red Mirror,
the enchanted head of the people
many times decapitated
bouncing from milpa to street
with looted eyes extorted ears
thoughts defrauded by the Scorpion
with more than 60 legs and a tail
packed with decades of poison.

I'm speaking to your hips and
your shoulders, O ballplayers and warriors,
bouncing from one neck to another,
telling over and over—with variations
of lips grimaces cries grumbles and groans—
how the Nafta New Order is lethal gas
intended to turn our land into a death chamber,
how it is a crusher of the intestines
of squash, a dirty smear of smog, ash

and grated pesos on tortillas to eat and die from,
and the stinking up of the sweet potato
thighs and the lip-biting flowers.

I'm censing from this pot of rage
on this trivet of stones on a sidestreet
of a Mayanalan slum,

I'm speaking to gums that no longer have teeth
(PRI has yanked them),
to teeth that no longer have gold
(PRI has stolen it),
to bones starving under layers of rags,
to rachitic chests, to gangrene, to pneumonia,
to the whole Commune Deficiency System which
PRI has depleted, poisoned and thrown away
like tripe in a supermercado garbage-can.

The chocolate skeleton from Tenantzingo
to Mescaltepec is exhorting you,
O ballplayers O warriors—
Xilotl Xilotl emerging ears of corn
Listen Listen for the movement
of living glyphs and stelae in the jungle!
They have embraced They have united
despite the abrasions of injustice and fraud

Listen to the copal's whirling messengers
The Fire opening its mouth The Tree pouring forth
O plume of People's Oil touched by the word
all true men and women live for!

O spurt of flame from the guts of deepest hungers!
O tongue of the Incendiary Serpent,
we will be with you tomorrow when we strike!

1996

WHATEVER IT'S CALLED

I snow before my time
I cover the pockmarked streets
with the black breaths of my birthday
I know why it is best
and why the valley is radiant

There's an old woman on that corner
holding out a pack of cigarets
that she's got from a man
for her shawl
who got it from a thief
for a bicycle part
who stole it from the pocket
of an American businessman
who's arranging to build
a computer parts factory
on the outskirts of Moscow

She is all rags
Her hand is out
I fall on her shabby coat
on her nose on her eyelashes

In a room across the street
a man of 50 just stops breathing
in his chair

A cheap little samovar
of a woman clips her stocking
to her garter, smoothes down her dress,
sprays some blackmarket perfume
on her neck and goes downstairs
to walk the streets

Her heels are what's left
of the Red Army

I bury her on a thousand corners
and freeze her and her sisters
into statues

My name was changed long ago
She is my name, and the man
in the room no longer breathing,
and the old woman who sells
stolen cigarets

I snow, even in the room
I bury him in my black breaths

This is the true *Requiem*.
Slava to the victorious revolution
Stalingrad or whatever it's called
is triumphant

I fall and fall I slowly cover all
with my black breaths.

1996

SOMETHING BASIC

for LOCAL 87 AFL-CIO

Something basic like night
when sleepers are unaware their nightmares
are being swept away so their dreams can
put on their best,

when the dust of yesterday's deals
is cleared from the four corners of office
machines sleeping with one eye open.

Something basic like giant
moustaches of brooms sweeping across
the sidewalks of childhood, through schoolrooms
and libraries so that even old books feel
spanking new.

Someone basic as a fuse
in the cellar of a tenement darkened by lightning,
one who makes sure water comes out of the faucets,
maintains the necessary order of things at the highest
level of discrete invisibility, like simplicity itself,
is often the indigenous immigrant at the root

of what makes the whole show continue,
the human janitor, who must not be slashed
like a throwaway book by the cut-crazy backstabbers
of the people, the he or she who is the real
governor of the state of things
still possibly human.

1996

THE RECOGNITION #2

I know it was her
Sigourney
I turned my head
upside in the darkness
just after the Nazis
were forced by the liberating army
to throw her dead body
into the pit — yes,
it was the same face, it was
Sigourney,
her breasts strangely still fleshed
though below them
just a clacking skeleton
of thigh-bones and stick-legs

I'd never seen this footage before
—perhaps because it was Russian—
so I'd never seen Sigourney — yes,
it was Sigourney Weaver
before she had even been born,
but that's impossible,
but nothing *is* after that period,

I'm telling you it was Sigourney Weaver
who went plummeting onto the pile
—her face her hair her torso—
to a shuddering violin-bow,
it was unmistakeably Sigourney
and I understood
why I loved Sigourney Weaver
without ever having seen her in a film,
from just having caught a momentary
glimpse of her in an interview,
she began entering my fantasies,
not however as a star,
I never saw her as a star,
nor had seen her work as a star,
in fact what I loved about her
was that she didn't come off
as a star, she came off as . . .
I didn't know. . . I didn't know. . .
a woman, of course . . . an ordinary woman

but I didn't know why or wherefrom
and couldn't believe a few-seconds
image in an interview could have
so deeply and for some years
penetrated my very being

until last night when I saw her
in that mass pit, and there
was no mistaking: it was Sigourney,
and if you don't believe
what I'm getting at, just look
around, down the street, across
the way, across the drink,
just you look outside.

1996

THE OPEN GATE

In Memory of Jack Micheline

When I came to San Francisco
the street was Jack.
I write this on the #19 as it passes
the now non-existent *Donuts 'n' Things*
on Polk and California Streets
where during the war we talked
of poets here and in the Soviet Union
before going to Minnie Can Do's
over on Fillmore to do our things,
or headed to North Beach for
the wild venues there.

Later I learned the street was more
than Jack. It was jack, and few of us
had much of it; and we saw poor
palms opening everywhere, the war
had broken many, and the rats in power,
and the cockroach landlords.

Jack lived for the walk,
for the open gate inside

where the prisoner hears the strain
of Mingus or Monk, and sings free
along the storefronts and to
the windows of the world.

The bohemian was dead but he said:
Long Live the Bohemian!
The poets were canned or clowned
or given microphones to suck on
but he cried: Long Live the Poets!

Those he envied and decried for having
made it beat in the literary world
he was right about: they really
weren't street, and street was where
the Poet had to be, or street would be
ruled by dead spores and fascisti.
He had a memory,
a bottle of chianti,
a gypsy-jewish fire burning in him
all the way back to Black Pushkin,
had the con the hustle the scrounge the wail
to survive in a world where blood money
rigged up everybody's sails,

all that to keep the gate open inside
for the poem to blow as a hurricane,
for the paint to animal and child.

Old buddy of the Word, those guts you kept
like a holy ark of sparks bursting into flame
you pass on into all of us now bereft
—the hip, the dudes, the chicks, the dames—

We ask a doll, we ask a dish, Rimbaud,
Mayakovsky, Kerouac and all
the streethearts gathered here:
wasn't that a matzoh in the teeth of homeless fate?
wasn't that a Poet made of bright and shining tears?

1998

POEM FOR THE MILLENNIUM

Amid history's dust,
among vestigial bones of old ideologies,
one foot forward but seemingly no way forward or back
and originary thinking a dream beating its head
against a computer screen that's already
infomercialed it,

some see the Millennium as billions
of people in need, some as billions
of bux; some see the gap widening between
haves and have-nots, some see the Gap
globally expanding . . . its shops.

How to get a roof over everyone's head?
How to get 3 squares for all, ad infinitum?

There's more terror. More greed.
More wraparound cars.
More thugs and scorpions
disguised in democracy.
More wars. More cops. More poor,
more poor, more
poor and homeless   .

masses in rags,
garbage-pickers, panhandlers, whores.
More mass-graves, slave-labor payoff promises,
arms unsleeving in Needle Alleys,
swarms of tourists passing by.

Death, you tear out our hearts and say,
See, they're only muscles!
and feed 'em to the sun of profits.
Death, we're up to here in your blood-works
and have had enough of the back-break
and shell-game that hustles us dry.

We're sick of this destiny of exploitation
and want another kind of society,
and can have, and will.

The bottom line moved in Seattle
almost 7 years since LA
on a wider stage
40,000 workers with environmentalists
internationally strong
and the kick-ass of the New Class
screwing the tear-gas and the jails
raising the spiral song
against the negation

that is capital.

And now we can and will
put more poor-sparks to those aglow
on every wrong, together making
a Millennium fire that will spread
our desire for a world co-operatively tuned
like an instrument all people will have
a hand in the making and playing of,

to get the whole body of soul back,
and the dignity nailed to the garbage pail,
and the faces ripped off and the feelings killed,
and be able at last to walk out of every moment's jail
into a world where a piece of bread
will profitlessly belong to all,
and where you'll come to a door no longer a stranger
and find the place is yours simply because you're human,
and free as well the schools and hospitals
for you to live your heart out
the way it was meant to beat.

2000
67

THE LOVE POEM

for Aggiemou

Bliss of all blisses
lightly you do declare
intimacy by putting your
lips right here.

So *this* is thought
without itself! Spoken though
nothing's said, nothing when
it's everything, naked

kiss that's shed the crumbs
of time and the orgy
of pennies thrown
and stuck to the mind

and now, alone with one
of a kind pair of lips,
the origin of itself opens
in order to reveal:

there *is* a language called

Soul, a tongue that is
the kiss that's the bliss
of all blisses. Untranslatable.

2000

THE WHOLE SHOT

In Memory of Gregory Corso

Most, given the death we've all been given
before we die, die.
Greg didn't, Greg wouldn't, Greg ain't.
He burned his being burned and being burned up
right in front of you,
up front,
in your face, he was a fighting little neighborhood,
city-wide.

I never saw him sing, he never sang, copper,
O but he sang.
And guzzled and fixed and trashed and mashed.
Consumed. He was consumed by consuming,
competition's fool,
from Maldoror through every lowdown kind of
kinahoor clear down to his own stretch-marks
in Dannemora.

I went to see him in the hospital once
when his head, 3 times its size, some blood

he'd dissed in the drunk-tank had kicked in.
Which was after he'd once right-crossed me
for no good reason, like my best friend the
Calabrese kid in my neighborhood in The Bronx.
Which was before a bull-dyke once decked him
for dissing lesbians, and for being monstrously cute,
humiliating in public to women and men alike,
a self-styled "rotten fuck" who never cleaned up,
a nice guy who said, "No more nice guy",
all brag and loudmouth blow,
fame up his ass
"I'm Gregory Corso"
like at a horseshow,

provoking, stirring shit,
yelling, "Hey, Ginzy!" up to Shig's place on Grant St.
when Allen was visiting, for some dough.
Or: "Hey, Jackie, where's Neeli? He took
Max for a walk . . ."

In this bar or that, running with this or that mug,
that chick or this,
toking in an alley or back in the john,
or cross-legged serious in the Caffe Trieste
reading the Chronicle or The Times

mixing it up with a mouth in a gallop
like Billy Hallop,
with twinkle and charm out of hell,
he was one of a kind
of a devil character,

so you might never have known
he could precision an image
to its finest fain,
turn a phrase and make it sit in
with a combo of sounds
that unearthed a flagrant poesy
from ancient undergrounds,
write from a spring
without himself in it
and make the running diamonds
"the whole ball game",
or "the stiff arm of Cuba"
more than just sport,
"the whole shot"
in the senses that toppled
lying news reports,
taking one's breath away
and leaving a real agape suddenly
sprouting daisies in your empty spaces,

the way it is when you're met
by a pair of eyes on the street
above a mouth that might say anything,
above a body that might do anything,

yet those eyes in a slow, smiling
recognition rise and wink:
"Hey you, human bean, you Poet,
you synechdochal yokel of All,
Nothing's concealed,
Nothing's hid.
Cross my heart and hope to live."

The Kid is dead.
Long Live the Kid!

2001

THE HAPPINESS

There's a happiness, a joy
in the soul, that's been
buried alive in everyone
and forgotten.

It isn't your barroom joke
or tender, intimate humor
or affections of friendliness
or a big, bright pun.

They're the surviving survivors
of what happened when happiness
was buried alive, when
it no longer looked out

of today's eyes, and doesn't
even manifest when one
of us dies, we just walk away
from everything, alone

with what's left of us,
going on being human beings
without being human,
without that happiness.

2001

THE TWIN TOWERS ARCANE

1.

Such mourning as we
might wake from
(having been woken from by such a light)
to see the light
at last:

that we are now
no more
nor less
      but have been more than others

a violent land

in our money markets
in our law 'n' orders
in our daily Dailies
in our beds

a violent life

pretending to an impenetrable innocence
and power symbolized

by those giant
Twins.

Their destruction:
Hitler's dream, dreamed before
they even were built,
before his suicide
began to fight on the side
of religious fanaticism.

And we
who had inherited so much
of his violence and anti-communism,
we who've even ultimately
financed the attack
on our pretended innocence
—we so at home
with fascism (denied, of course)
with brutality (foresworn, of course)
with liberty sentimentalized
from a core of destructive emptiness,
hopelessness,
cynicism at bottom,

children of a star-spangled
nihilism (of course denied and foresworn)

"from California
to the New York island"

brothers and sisters,
my own
so sadly struck,
so deeply struck.

2.

The Israeli says: "Now they know"
who himself has been infested
with genes
from the 12 year
long syringe of unforgettable evil.

Presumably it's we who now know
what it means to be totally detested
to the point of apocalypse.

And it's a fascist defense against
a fascist attack that the world
is preparing, for there's nothing
but that nothingness
of a scorpion planet eating
its own tail;

and it's the awareness of that truth
that doubles the mourning
and profounds the fear
of the loss of the innocence
that was a lie in the first place.

This time we're really trapped
by truth and it grieves us
who've been so comfortable
in the liberty of the lie.

This time the total mobilization
of war consciousness says:
even if pacifism grows,
even if it prevents responsive attacks,
even if non-violence triumphs,
the future will be
like a Black man who,
or like eroticism which,
while no longer lynched or censored,
will nevertheless never
feel altogether at home
in worldly life.

The rule of nothingness
is complete now.

God murdered on one hand.
God suicided on the other.

The triumph of fascism.

We're ordered to live out
our non-violent lives
buying and selling
and praying to violence
despite ourselves

because there's nothing else,
nothing's changed,
it's only standing more revealed.

3.

Celia,
I know you ran toward
not away from,
to help, to save.

And that you saw the
second plane evaporate
in the wall as you ran
toward.

And that you saw, for
the first time in your life,
human beings leaping
from the high ledges

and the Twins collapsing
into a single mountain
of thousand-fold death
and rubble and dust.

Nothing I was witness to
on a television screen
thousands of miles away
on another continent

can approach the horror
of what you saw as you
ran toward the scene
till you could no more,

dust-clouds billowing
through the streets and
those running for their
lives from the core

told you you could go

no further, couldn't help,
couldn't save, O my
brave, brave daughter.

I know your grief isn't
from afar. In vain, in vain
they died! you cry and
your despair there perhaps

spares, perhaps even saves
us from the shock which
turned the future into an
archaic archeological dig.

4.

The night that has arrived, the technological night, all day,
and with it mourning,
the fast of the fast,
the bitter taste
of one's own desert.

And that it is not only one's own
but that we're all speaking with mouths of sand,
and dunes are growing, undulating with the discourse
of a dazzling darkness in the sun

that is broken in each of us.

All night, airplanes and helicopters have been flying over
the burnt-sienna porticos of Bologna,
where I happen to be
mourning.
It's become the State
of Being.

A black flag
at half mast.

Hanging in mid-air.

2001

JACK HIRSCHMAN was born December 13, 1933 in The Bronx, New York. He worked as a reporter in his teens, as an academic in his twenties, and was dismissed as a teacher at UCLA in 1966 having broken state examination laws in his attempt to prevent students from being drafted into the Vietnam War. For the past 30 years he has lived in San Francisco and, for the past three years, each six months in England as well. He has published more than 100 books and chapbooks of poetry and essays, half of which are translations of poets from nine different languages. During those years he has worked with the Communist Labor Party, the Union of Left Writers, the Roque Dalton Cultural Brigade, the Jacques Roumain Cultural Brigade, and (currently) the League of Revolutionaries for a New America (LRNA), and *Left Curve* magazine. His books have been translated and published in Italy and France where, among other countries, he gives yearly readings. His paintings and other visual work are expressions as well of a prodigious creative life.

CITY LIGHTS PUBLICATIONS

Acosta, Juvenal, ed. LIGHT FROM A NEARBY WINDOW: Contemporary Mexican Poetry
Alberti, Rafael. CONCERNING THE ANGELS
Alcalay, Ammiel, ed. KEYS TO THE GARDEN: New Israeli Writing
Alcalay, Ammiel. MEMORIES OF OUR FUTURE: Selected Essays 1982-1999
Allen, Roberta. AMAZON DREAM
Angulo de, G. & J. JAIME IN TAOS
Angulo, Jaime de. INDIANS IN OVERALLS
Artaud, Antonin. ARTAUD ANTHOLOGY
Barker, Molly. SECRET LANGUAGE
Bataille, Georges. EROTISM: Death and Sensuality
Bataille, Georges. THE IMPOSSIBLE
Bataille, Georges. STORY OF THE EYE
Bataille, Georges. THE TEARS OF EROS
Baudelaire, Charles. TWENTY PROSE POEMS
Blanco, Alberto. DAWN OF THE SENSES: Selected Poems
Blechman, Max. REVOLUTIONARY ROMANTICISM
Bowles, Paul. A HUNDRED CAMELS IN THE COURTYARD
Bramly, Serge. MACUMBA: The Teachings of Maria-José, Mother of the Gods
Brecht, Bertolt. STORIES OF MR. KEUNER
Breton, André. ANTHOLOGY OF BLACK HUMOR
Brook, James, Chris Carlsson, Nancy J. Peters eds. RECLAIMING SAN FRANCISCO: History Politics Culture
Brook, James & Iain A. Boal. RESISTING THE VIRTUAL LIFE: Culture and Politics of Information
Broughton, James. COMING UNBUTTONED
Brown, Rebecca. ANNIE OAKLEY'S GIRL
Brown, Rebecca. THE DOGS
Brown, Rebecca. THE TERRIBLE GIRLS
Bukowski, Charles. THE MOST BEAUTIFUL WOMAN IN TOWN
Bukowski, Charles. NOTES OF A DIRTY OLD MAN
Bukowski, Charles. TALES OF ORDINARY MADNESS
Burroughs, William S. THE BURROUGHS FILE
Burroughs, William S. THE YAGE LETTERS
Campana, Dino. ORPHIC SONGS
Cassady, Neal. THE FIRST THIRD
Chin, Sara. BELOW THE LINE
Churchill, Ward. FANTASIES OF THE MASTER RACE: Literature, Cinema and the Colonization of American Indians
Churchill, Ward. A LITTLE MATTER OF GENOCIDE: Holocaust and Denial in America, 1492 to the Present
Cocteau, Jean. THE WHITE BOOK (LE LIVRE BLANC)
Cohen, Jonathan. APART FROM FREUD: Notes for a Rational Psychoanalysis
Cornford, Adam. ANIMATIONS
Corso, Gregory. GASOLINE
Cortázar, Julio. SAVE TWILIGHT
Cuadros, Gil. CITY OF GOD

Daumal, René. THE POWERS OF THE WORD
David-Neel, Alexandra. SECRET ORAL TEACHINGS IN TIBETAN BUDDHIST SECTS
Deleuze, Gilles. SPINOZA: Practical Philosophy
Dick, Leslie. KICKING
Dick, Leslie. WITHOUT FALLING
di Prima, Diane. PIECES OF A SONG: Selected Poems
Doolittle, Hilda (H.D.). NOTES ON THOUGHT & VISION
Ducornet, Rikki. ENTERING FIRE
Ducornet, Rikki. THE MONSTROUS AND THE MARVELOUS
Dunbar-Ortiz, Roxanne. OUTLAW WOMAN: A Memoir of the War Years 1960–1975
Eberhardt, Isabelle. DEPARTURES: Selected Writings
Eberhardt, Isabelle. THE OBLIVION SEEKERS
Eidus, Janice. THE CELIBACY CLUB
Eidus, Janice. URBAN BLISS
Eidus, Janice. VITO LOVES GERALDINE
Fenollosa, Ernest. THE CHINESE WRITTEN CHARACTER AS A MEDIUM FOR POETRY
Ferlinghetti, L. ed. CITY LIGHTS POCKET POETS ANTHOLOGY
Ferlinghetti, L., ed. ENDS & BEGINNINGS (City Lights Review #6)
Ferlinghetti, L. PICTURES OF THE GONE WORLD
Finley, Karen. SHOCK TREATMENT
Ford, Charles Henri. OUT OF THE LABYRINTH: Selected Poems
Franzen, Cola, transl. POEMS OF ARAB ANDALUSIA
Frym, Gloria. DISTANCE NO OBJECT
García Lorca, Federico. BARBAROUS NIGHTS: Legends & Plays
García Lorca, Federico. ODE TO WALT WHITMAN & OTHER POEMS
García Lorca, Federico. POEM OF THE DEEP SONG
Garon, Paul. BLUES & THE POETIC SPIRIT
Gil de Biedma, Jaime. LONGING: SELECTED POEMS
Ginsberg, Allen. THE FALL OF AMERICA
Ginsberg, Allen. HOWL & OTHER POEMS
Ginsberg, Allen. KADDISH & OTHER POEMS
Ginsberg, Allen. MIND BREATHS
Ginsberg, Allen. PLANET NEWS
Ginsberg, Allen. PLUTONIAN ODE
Ginsberg, Allen. REALITY SANDWICHES
Glave, Thomas. WHOSE SONG? And Other Stories
Goethe, J. W. von. TALES FOR TRANSFORMATION
Gómez-Peña, Guillermo. THE NEW WORLD BORDER
Gómez-Peña, Guillermo, Enrique Chagoya, Felicia Rice. CODEX ESPANGLIENSIS
Goytisolo, Juan. LANDSCAPES OF WAR
Goytisolo. Juan. THE MARX FAMILY SAGA
Guillén, Jorge. HORSES IN THE AIR AND OTHER POEMS
Hagedorn, Jessica. DANGER AND BEAUTY
Hammond, Paul. CONSTELLATIONS OF MIRÓ, BRETON
Hammond, Paul. THE SHADOW AND ITS SHADOW: Surrealist Writings on Cinema
Harryman, Carla. THERE NEVER WAS A ROSE WITHOUT A THORN
Herron, Don. THE DASHIELL HAMMETT TOUR: A Guidebook

Pasolini, Pier Paolo. ROMAN POEMS
Pessoa, Fernando. ALWAYS ASTONISHED
Pessoa, Fernando. POEMS OF FERNANDO PESSOA
Poe, Edgar Allan. THE UNKNOWN POE
Porta, Antonio. KISSES FROM ANOTHER DREAM
Prévert, Jacques. PAROLES
Purdy, James. THE CANDLES OF YOUR EYES
Purdy, James. GARMENTS THE LIVING WEAR
Purdy, James. IN A SHALLOW GRAVE
Purdy, James. OUT WITH THE STARS
Rachlin, Nahid. THE HEART'S DESIRE
Rachlin, Nahid. MARRIED TO A STRANGER
Rachlin, Nahid. VEILS: SHORT STORIES
Reed, Jeremy. DELIRIUM: An Interpretation of Arthur Rimbaud
Reed, Jeremy. RED-HAIRED ANDROID
Rey Rosa, Rodrigo. THE BEGGAR'S KNIFE
Rey Rosa, Rodrigo. DUST ON HER TONGUE
Rigaud, Milo. SECRETS OF VOODOO
Rodríguez, Artemio and Herrera, Juan Felipe. LOTERIA CARDS AND FORTUNE POEMS
Ross, Dorien. RETURNING TO A
Ruy Sánchez, Alberto. MOGADOR
Saadawi, Nawal El. MEMOIRS OF A WOMAN DOCTOR
Sawyer-Lauçanno, Christopher. THE CONTINUAL PILGRIMAGE: American Writers in Paris 1944-1960
Sawyer-Lauçanno, Christopher, transl. THE DESTRUCTION OF THE JAGUAR
Scholder, Amy, ed. CRITICAL CONDITION: Women on the Edge of Violence
Schelling, Andrew, tr. CANE GROVES OF NARMADA RIVER: Erotic Poems from Old India
Serge, Victor. RESISTANCE
Shepard, Sam. MOTEL CHRONICLES
Shepard, Sam. FOOL FOR LOVE & THE SAD LAMENT OF PECOS BILL
Solnit, Rebecca. SECRET EXHIBITION: Six California Artists
Tabucchi, Antonio. DREAMS OF DREAMS and THE LAST THREE DAYS OF FERNANDO PESSOA
Takahashi, Mutsuo. SLEEPING SINNING FALLING
Turyn, Anne, ed. TOP TOP STORIES
Tutuola, Amos. SIMBI & THE SATYR OF THE DARK JUNGLE
Ulin, David L., ed. ANOTHER CITY: WRITING FROM LOS ANGELES
Ullman, Ellen. CLOSE TO THE MACHINE: Technophilia and Its Discontents
Valaoritis, Nanos. MY AFTERLIFE GUARANTEED
VandenBroeck, André. BREAKING THROUGH
Vega, Janine Pommy. TRACKING THE SERPENT
Veltri, George. NICE BOY
Waldman, Anne. FAST SPEAKING WOMAN
Wilson, Colin. POETRY AND MYSTICISM
Wilson, John. INK ON PAPER: Poems on Chinese & Japanese Paintings
Wilson, Peter Lamborn. PLOUGHING THE CLOUDS
Wilson, Peter Lamborn. SACRED DRIFT
Wynne, John. THE OTHER WORLD
Zamora, Daisy. RIVERBED OF MEMORY